Canon EOS R1 User Guide

Step by Step Pro Setups, Autofocus Mastery & Real-World Shooting Recipes (Sports, Wildlife, Events & Video)

Randy Osborn

Disclaimer & Non-Affiliation

This book is an independent resource created for photographers and videographers who wish to maximize the potential of their Canon EOS R1 camera. It is designed to provide practical, field-tested guidance, shooting recipes, and workflow strategies that go beyond the scope of the official instruction manual.

Canon, EOS, and R1 are trademarks of Canon Inc. and/or its affiliates. All references to these names and product designations in this book are made strictly for descriptive and educational purposes only. The author and publisher are not affiliated with, sponsored by, endorsed by, or connected in any way to Canon Inc. or any of its subsidiaries.

This publication is not an official Canon manual. Readers who require Canon's official technical documentation, safety warnings, or warranty information should consult the materials provided with the camera or visit Canon's official website.

While every effort has been made to ensure accuracy at the time of writing—including references to current firmware, common configurations, and tested shooting techniques—camera technology evolves. Canon may release firmware updates, new features, or additional accessories that could alter or enhance the functionality of the EOS R1. Readers are encouraged to stay current with Canon's updates and adapt the guidance provided here as needed.

Important: The techniques, settings, and workflows described in this book are based on professional field use and represent the author's recommendations. However, results will vary depending on shooting conditions, personal style, and equipment choices. The author and publisher assume no responsibility for damages, malfunctions, or missed photographic opportunities that may arise from the application of this material. Use all equipment responsibly and within the safety and operational guidelines provided by Canon Inc.

By reading this book, you acknowledge that it is an independent educational guide and that Canon Inc. retains full ownership of its intellectual property, brand names, and trademarks.

How to Use This Book

The Canon EOS R1 is a flagship camera with incredible depth—but with that power comes complexity. If you've already glanced through the official manual, you know it's thorough, technical, and sometimes overwhelming. This book was written to serve a very different purpose.

Instead of walking you through every button and menu in sequence, it gives you a field roadmap: clear, practical guidance on how to configure the R1 for real-world shooting situations. Where the manual tells you *what* each function does, this guide shows you *why it matters* and *how to use it in practice*.

Think of the manual as your dictionary—precise, comprehensive, and technical. Think of this book as your field companion—direct, experience-driven, and focused on results.

- When you need manual info: you'll get plain-language explanations of key features (like Eye-Controlled Autofocus or Pre-Shooting Burst) so you understand what they do.

- When you want field recipes: you'll find step-by-step setups and scenario-based blueprints—"how to configure the camera for fast indoor sports," "how to track birds in flight," "how to manage 6K RAW video without overheating." These are designed to get you shooting confidently, not just studying settings.

To make it even easier, the book is structured with:

- Quick-Start Checklists to get you set up in under an hour.

- Pro Setup Maps that show how working photographers configure the camera.

- Shooting Recipes you can apply immediately to sports, wildlife, events, and video work.

- Firmware Notes to keep you current with Canon's updates.

- Field Cards in the back for fast reference when you're out on location.

You don't need to read cover to cover in one sitting. Start with the Quick-Start, then dive into the sections that match your shooting style. Over time, return to the recipes and workflow chapters as you expand into new genres.

This way, the EOS R1 becomes less of a complicated machine and more of a trusted partner—an extension of your eye, instincts, and creative intent.

Fast-Start Checklist

What to Set Up in the First 30 Minutes Before Your First Shoot

Unboxing the Canon EOS R1 is exciting—but staring at its menus can be daunting. Instead of diving into every option, start here. In half an hour, you'll have a camera that's ready for real shooting, with the most important foundations dialed in.

1. Power & Media Essentials

- Insert a fully charged battery (or two if you own the grip).
- Load your CFexpress Type B card(s)—format them in-camera for a clean start.
- Set your file type: RAW + JPEG (or RAW + HEIF if you want efficiency).

2. Date, Time & File Organization

- Set your date, time, and timezone—critical for event coverage.

- Change file numbering to continuous so you don't reset with every card.

- Rename custom folders if you want to separate shoots (sports, wildlife, jobs).

3. Basic Exposure Defaults

- Shooting mode: Manual (M) for control or Aperture Priority (Av) for fast-paced work.

- ISO: Set to Auto ISO with a max cap around 6400 for most work.

- Exposure comp: Enable rear dial quick adjustment for fast fixes.

4. Autofocus Setup

- Enable Eye-Controlled AF and go through the calibration steps.

- Default AF area: Whole Area Tracking (lets you cover 90% of shooting).

- Register a secondary AF point (like a single spot) on a custom button.

5. Drive & Burst

- Continuous shooting mode: H+ (High-Speed Electronic) for sports/wildlife.

- Enable Pre-Shooting Burst if you expect fast, unpredictable action.

- Silent shutter: turn ON for events or OFF if you prefer audible confirmation.

6. Image Stabilization & Lens Communication

- Activate IBIS + lens IS for combined stabilization.

- For super-telephoto lenses, check mode (Standard vs. Panning) and set accordingly.

7. White Balance & Color

- Default WB: Auto (Ambience Priority) unless under LED or mixed light.

- Picture Style: Set to Neutral for RAW workflow or Standard for JPEG delivery.

- Video shooters: enable Canon Log (C-Log 2 or 3) if grading later.

8. Custom Buttons & My Menu

- Assign back-button focus (AF-ON) for reliability.

- Map your rate button to switch AF methods quickly.

- Add your top 5 menu items (format card, silent shutter, AF area, ISO range, log on/off) to My Menu.

9. Video Basics (if hybrid shooting)

- Recording format: 4K HQ for quality, 4K 60p/120p for action, or 6K RAW if your workflow supports it.

- Assign a dedicated record button for muscle memory.

- Check record limit & card space before rolling.

10. Save & Backup

- Save your current setup to a Custom Shooting Mode (C1, C2, C3).

- Create one each for Sports/Wildlife, Events, and Video—you'll refine them later.

- Back up settings to card, so firmware updates don't wipe them.

Field-Ready in 30 Minutes

Once you've walked through this checklist, your R1 will be more than just powered on—it will be field-configured. You won't capture every nuance yet, but you'll be able to walk into a stadium, forest, or wedding hall and start working with confidence.

From here, the chapters ahead will help you deepen each setup into a specialized recipe—whether that means eye-control AF for sports, long-lens tracking for birds in flight, or hybrid video rigs for demanding shoots.

Table of Contents

Preface

The Canon EOS R1 is more than just a flagship canon mirrorless camera—it is a professional workhorse built for speed, accuracy, and creativity. Whether you are just starting out and looking for a canon eos r1 for beginners or you are an established photographer searching for a canon eos r1 practical guide, this comprehensive canon eos r1 user guide takes you from setup to mastery with ease.

Inside, you'll find step-by-step instruction presented in clear, real-world language. The book doubles as both a canon eos r1 manual and a hands-on canon eos r1 photography guide, covering everything from the exposure triangle with canon eos to advanced autofocus mastery canon eos techniques. You'll learn how to make the most of canon eye-controlled autofocus, refine your skills with the canon burst shooting guide, and take control of light through canon exposure and metering strategies.

For action shooters, the canon eos r1 sports photography section shows how to configure the ultimate canon sports camera setup, complete with canon sports lens pairing advice and proven canon camera shooting recipes. Wildlife lovers will appreciate the detailed canon eos r1 wildlife photography walkthrough, with practical canon wildlife tracking tips and canon wildlife lens tips that ensure sharp, breathtaking images in the field.

Event specialists will benefit from the canon event photography guide, as well as targeted chapters on canon wedding videography guide techniques, canon concert video tips, and strategies for news coverage and documentary assignments. Each scenario includes a ready-to-use canon eos r1 setup guide and quick-reference shooting recipes handbook so you never miss the moment.

Video creators will find this book equally indispensable. From canon eos r1 video settings and canon eos r1 6k raw video to canon eos r1 4k 120p settings, you'll discover how to choose between formats and build a workflow around them. Learn about canon

canon log setup, canon eos r1 video workflow strategies, and how to construct hybrid rigs with the canon hybrid rig guide. If your goal is to master canon cinematic setup guide techniques, this is your essential canon eos r1 video guide.

Practical tools such as best canon r1 lenses recommendations, canon eos r1 memory card setup instructions, and canon r1 battery management tips save you costly mistakes. You'll also learn how to integrate tethering with the canon tethering guide, design a secure canon file workflow setup, and apply a smart canon camera backup strategy. With guidance on canon eos r1 firmware updates and the most reliable canon eos r1 professional accessories, your system remains future-ready.

Whether you identify as a hobbyist seeking a canon eos r1 guide for seniors, a newcomer wanting a canon camera photography for beginners approach, or a working shooter needing an advanced canon photography guide, this canon eos r1 field guide delivers. It doubles as a canon eos r1 reference book and a canon pro workflow book—one you can return to before every important job.

The lessons here include canon professional shooting guide insights, mirrorless sports photography tips, wildlife photography with canon step-by-steps, and canon professional video setup breakdowns. You'll explore canon autofocus case studies, see the best settings for canon r1 across genres, and unlock the nuances of canon r1 shooting modes explained with clarity.

This isn't just another manual—it's the ultimate professional canon photography resource designed to turn your Canon EOS R1 into an extension of your vision. If you want pro canon camera tips combined with the confidence of a canon eos r1 reference book, this guide is your key to shooting smarter, faster, and better in every environment.

Introduction

The Canon EOS R1 is not just another camera. It represents the culmination of decades of Canon's engineering, a flagship body designed to deliver speed, precision, and reliability at the highest level of professional photography and video. Whether you are shooting the split-second expression of an athlete at the finish line, tracking a bird against a stormy sky, or capturing once-in-a-lifetime wedding vows under unpredictable lighting, the EOS R1 is built to meet those demands.

And yet—owning the most advanced camera in the world doesn't automatically translate into stronger images. The real challenge is unlocking the potential of the machine and integrating it seamlessly into your workflow, vision, and instinct as a shooter. That's where this book comes in.

Beyond the Manual

Canon provides an official instruction manual that covers every button, menu item, and specification. It's thorough, but it's not meant to teach you how to think like a photographer under pressure. The manual can tell you what "Pre-Shooting Burst" does, but it won't explain how to set it up for capturing a football quarterback's release. It can list the AF Cases, but it won't show you which ones help you lock onto a bird weaving through treetops at dusk.

This guide was written to bridge that gap. It's not a rephrased manual. It's a field-oriented roadmap that distills the EOS R1's complexity into practical strategies and scenario-based recipes you can apply immediately.

Why This Book Exists

The truth is simple: the EOS R1 is a pro tool. But many photographers—even seasoned ones—feel overwhelmed when first navigating its dense menus, customizations, and autofocus capabilities. I've spoken with shooters who left powerful features untouched simply because they didn't know when or how to use them. This book was created to solve that problem.

Inside, you'll find:

- Fast-start checklists to configure your R1 in minutes.

- Autofocus mastery guides, including how to harness Eye-Controlled AF and AF Cases for real-world subjects.

- Field-tested shooting recipes for sports, wildlife, events, and professional video.

- Workflow strategies for managing files, tethering, and adapting to firmware updates.

- Practical insights you won't find in Canon's manual, drawn from real shooting environments rather than lab conditions.

Who This Book Is For

- Sports photographers who need to capture the decisive moment without missing a beat.

- Wildlife shooters who demand reliable tracking for unpredictable subjects.

- Event and documentary professionals who must adapt to rapidly changing light and situations.

- Hybrid creators who push the EOS R1 for both stills and cinematic video.

- And even ambitious enthusiasts who may not yet shoot for a living but want to master their craft with the best tool available.

If you've invested in an EOS R1, you're serious about your work. This book is designed to respect that seriousness by delivering professional-grade knowledge in a way that's practical, clear, and immediately usable.

How to Get the Most Out of This Book

You don't have to read every chapter in order. Start with the Fast-Start Checklist to get your camera ready within the first half hour. From there, skip ahead to the sections most relevant to your shooting style—sports, wildlife, events, or video. As your needs grow, circle back to the customization, workflow, and firmware chapters to deepen your mastery.

Treat this book like you would a trusted colleague in the field: someone who can show you what works, save you time, and help you capture the images that matter most.

The Bigger Picture

The Canon EOS R1 is more than a piece of gear. It's a partner that, when set up correctly, extends your vision and responsiveness. It disappears in your hands so you can focus on what truly matters: the story unfolding in front of your lens. My goal in writing this guide is not just to help you "learn the camera," but to help you own it—to make the R1 an extension of your instincts as a photographer.

So charge your batteries, format your cards, and turn the page. Let's take the Canon EOS R1 out of the manual and into the field, where it belongs.

Part I: Foundation for Professionals

Chapter 1

The EOS R1 Mindset: A Flagship Built for Speed & Precision

The Flagship Difference

When Canon announced the EOS R1, it wasn't just another entry in the R-series—it was the long-awaited flagship that sits at the very top of Canon's mirrorless lineup. To appreciate this camera fully, you must see it not as an incremental upgrade from the R5, R6, or even the R3, but as a body designed to redefine what speed, autofocus intelligence, and reliability mean for working professionals.

The R5 gave us resolution and hybrid flexibility. The R6 gave us affordability and low-light strength. The R3 pushed speed and autofocus further into the mirrorless era. But the R1 exists in a different category. This is the camera you pick up when the shot cannot be missed—whether that's an Olympic sprinter breaking a record, a bald eagle's talons striking water, or a once-in-a-lifetime wedding kiss.

The difference isn't in just one feature. It's in the combination:

- Unmatched autofocus intelligence, including eye-controlled AF that makes the camera feel like it's reading your intent.

- Pre-shooting burst capture, giving you images from before you even pressed the shutter.

- Incredible processing power that keeps up with every burst without slowing.

- Rugged build quality that can handle dust, rain, and extreme environments without flinching.

This is what separates the R1 from the R5, R6, or R3. It's not about what's "better" in spec sheets—it's about having a machine that is always ahead of you, never holding you back.

Canon's "Pro DNA" Design

Canon designed the R1 with a philosophy that has been consistent across its legendary flagship line: still photography first, with uncompromised video capabilities integrated seamlessly.

For decades, Canon's flagship bodies—the EOS-1D series—were trusted on sidelines, in press pits, and in wildlife blinds. The R1 inherits that DNA, reimagined for the mirrorless age. What does that mean in practice?

1. **Stills-first mentality**

   o Every control, every dial, every customizable button is tuned for the photographer who must react instantly. Nothing feels like a compromise or buried deep in a menu.

   o Autofocus performance is prioritized over everything else, because in the field, missing focus means missing history.

2. **Hybrid capability, not hybrid compromise**

- The R1 is not a "video camera that also takes stills." Nor is it "a stills camera that happens to do video." It's both, without friction.

- You can move from photographing a penalty kick to recording 6K RAW footage of the celebration without switching gear.

3. **Reliability over novelty**

- Canon doesn't experiment with flagship bodies—they deliver tried, tested tools. When you pick up an R1, you know it was built for professionals who don't have the luxury of gear failure.

This "pro DNA" is what makes the R1 a workhorse, not just a showcase of specs. And when you adopt the R1, you adopt that mindset: to be ready for anything, and to expect your camera to keep pace with you.

Pro Reliability: Cards, Batteries & Lenses

Owning an R1 is an investment, and like every flagship camera, its potential can only be unlocked with the right supporting gear. Choosing wisely here ensures the camera delivers consistent performance when it matters most.

Memory Cards: The Unsung Heroes

- The EOS R1 pushes incredible data rates. To keep up, CFexpress Type B cards are mandatory for high-speed bursts and 6K RAW video.
- Choose cards from reliable brands rated for sustained write speeds, not just peak numbers. A card that slows down mid-burst is the difference between capturing the winning goal and staring at a buffering light.
- Keep at least two high-capacity cards on hand. Professionals never rely on one.

Batteries: Powering Confidence

- The R1 uses Canon's LP-E19 battery system, a professional-grade cell designed for endurance.

- Carry spares—flagship performance draws flagship power. A wildlife shoot in winter or a sports tournament can drain more quickly than you expect.

- Always cycle and label your batteries. Reliability comes from preparation, not just capacity.

Lenses: Extending the Flagship's Vision

- The R1 will expose the weaknesses of subpar glass. Pair it with Canon's RF L-series lenses for sharpness, speed, and weather-sealing that matches the body.

- For sports: fast telephotos like the RF 100–300mm f/2.8L or RF 400mm f/2.8L.

- For wildlife: the RF 600mm f/4L or the more portable RF 100–500mm f/4.5–7.1L.

- For events: versatile zooms like the RF 24–70mm f/2.8L and RF 70–200mm f/2.8L.

- For video: primes with smooth focus breathing control, like the RF 50mm f/1.2L or RF Cine primes if your workflow justifies them.

Your supporting kit determines whether the R1 feels like a fully armed flagship—or an overpowered body hobbled by weak links.

The Mindset Moving Forward

To master the R1 is not simply to learn where every menu option lives. It's to adopt a mindset: your camera is no longer the limit—your vision, preparation, and instincts are.

This chapter is your foundation. From here, the book will take you into autofocus mastery, field shooting recipes, and workflow strategies. But remember this: the R1 is built for speed and precision, and when paired with the right gear and the right mindset, it becomes not just a tool, but an extension of you as a photographer.

EOS R1 Reliability

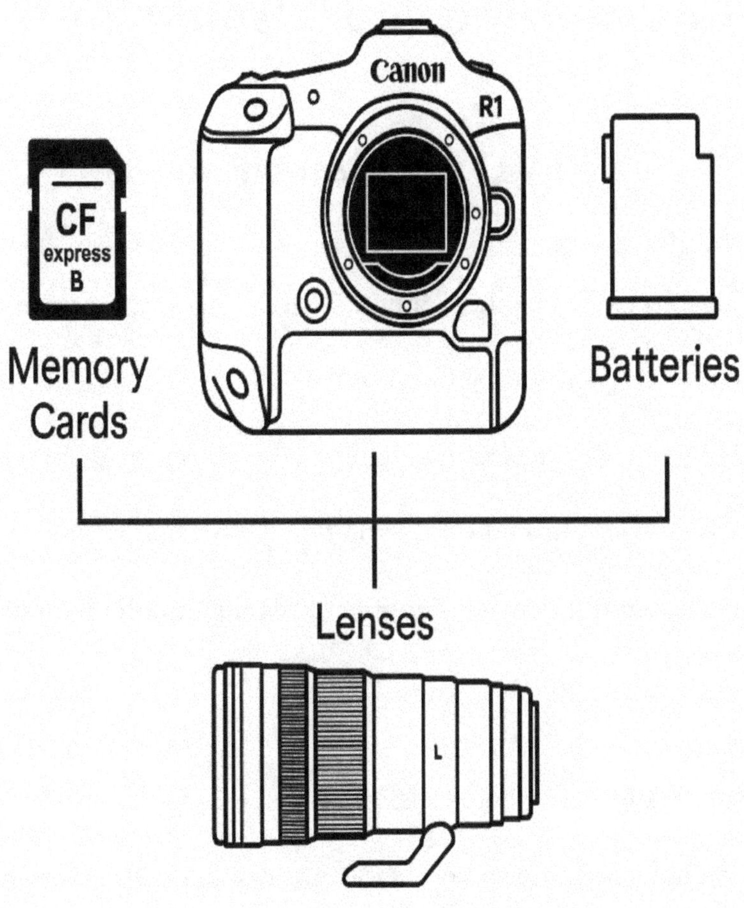

Chapter 2

Customizing Your Camera for You

Why Customization Matters

A flagship body like the Canon EOS R1 isn't just a camera—it's a system designed to bend to your style. Unlike entry-level or midrange models where the factory setup works "well enough," the R1 expects you to mold it. If you don't, you risk wasting precious time in menus or missing moments while fumbling for the right setting.

Customization is what transforms the R1 from a powerful but intimidating machine into a tool that responds as naturally as an extension of your own hand. In this chapter, we'll look at quick setup essentials, three levels of customization for different shooting needs, and practical, field-tested menu maps you can replicate immediately.

Quick Setup: Buttons, Dials & Menus Streamlined for Speed

The first layer of customization is simple: assigning the most critical functions to the buttons and dials you can reach without breaking eye contact with your subject.

- **Back-Button Focus (AF-ON):** Many pros swear by separating focus from the shutter. With the R1's deep AF capabilities, this setup prevents accidental refocusing and keeps tracking active only when you want it.

- **Rate Button Reassignment:** By default, this button rates images. Re-map it to toggle between AF methods (e.g., Wide AF vs. Single Point). This saves you from diving into menus mid-action.

- **Multi-Function (M-Fn) Button:** Place ISO or White Balance here for instant adjustment. During fast-paced shoots, exposure control belongs under your fingertips.

- **Dial Strategy:** Assign the main dial to shutter speed, quick dial to aperture, and rear wheel to ISO. Exposure becomes a seamless triangle you can adjust on the fly.

- **My Menu Setup:** Add your top 5 items—Format Card, Silent Shutter, AF Cases, Pre-Shooting Burst, and Log On/Off (for hybrid shooters). That single green tab becomes your efficiency hub.

With these quick adjustments, your R1 goes from "menu heavy" to "muscle memory."

Three Levels of Customization: Everyday, Sports & Video Rigs

The R1 shines when you configure it differently for different missions. The beauty of Custom Shooting Modes (C1, C2, C3) is that they let you build rigs inside the camera—no wrenching needed.

1. Everyday Rig (C1)

This is your walkaround, general-purpose setup.

- Mode: Aperture Priority (Av)

- AF: Whole Area Tracking, Eye Control enabled

- Drive: High-speed continuous, but not max (to conserve battery and card space)

- ISO: Auto, capped at 6400

- Custom Button: Rate button switches AF area from Wide to Single Spot

- Purpose: Daily work, portraits, street shooting, and casual assignments

2. Sports Rig (C2)

Here, speed and precision matter most.

- Mode: Manual Exposure, 1/2000s, f/2.8 baseline

- AF: Case 2 or Case 4 (tracking with acceleration/deceleration), Eye Control ON

- Drive: H+ electronic, Pre-Shooting Burst enabled

- ISO: Auto capped at 12800

- Custom Button: One touch to toggle between Servo AF with zone vs. Single Point for isolation

- Purpose: Indoor/outdoor field sports, unpredictable high-speed action

3. Video Rig (C3)

For hybrid shooters who need to pivot into cinema-grade output.

- Mode: Movie, C-Log 3 enabled

- Frame Rate: 4K 60p default, switchable to 6K RAW

- AF: Face/Eye Detect priority, with manual override mapped to AF-ON

- Audio: Levels set manually, limiter enabled

- Custom Button: Map Movie Rec to M-Fn for secondary trigger

- Purpose: Interviews, behind-the-scenes reels, or cinematic clips alongside stills

These rigs eliminate the need to rebuild settings before every assignment. Instead, you flick the mode dial and the R1 transforms instantly.

Field-Tested Menu Maps (Not Generic—Real Working Setups)

A camera this deep can overwhelm with choices, but professionals eventually boil them down into menu maps—a predictable structure where settings live where you expect them. Below are field-tested examples you can adopt and refine.

Sports Menu Map:

- Tab 1: AF Case Selection, Subject Detection (People vs. Animals), Eye Control Calibration

- Tab 2: Drive Mode (H+), Pre-Shooting Burst toggle, Electronic/Mechanical Shutter

- Tab 3: ISO Range Limits, Highlight Tone Priority, Anti-Flicker Shooting

Wildlife Menu Map:

- Tab 1: Eye Control Calibration (specific to your wildlife lens)

- Tab 2: Silent Shutter ON, IBIS settings tuned for long-lens stability

- Tab 3: Custom WB presets (forest shade, golden hour, overcast)

Video Menu Map:

- Tab 1: Movie Recording Quality (4K HQ / 6K RAW)

- Tab 2: C-Log ON/OFF, Zebras, Peaking

- Tab 3: Audio Levels, Timecode Sync, HDMI Output settings

The key here is consistency: once you decide where your most-used tools live, don't move them. This repetition builds the muscle memory that separates fumbling from fluency.

The Customization Mindset

Every great R1 user eventually realizes this truth: you don't adapt to the camera—the camera adapts to you. By taking the time to customize buttons, dials, and menus, you erase the distance between thought and action. That's when the camera becomes invisible— when all that's left is your subject and your vision.

This chapter sets you up for mastery by tailoring the R1 to your hands. In the next chapter, we'll go deeper into its beating heart: the autofocus system—and how to make it your ally, not your adversary, in the field.

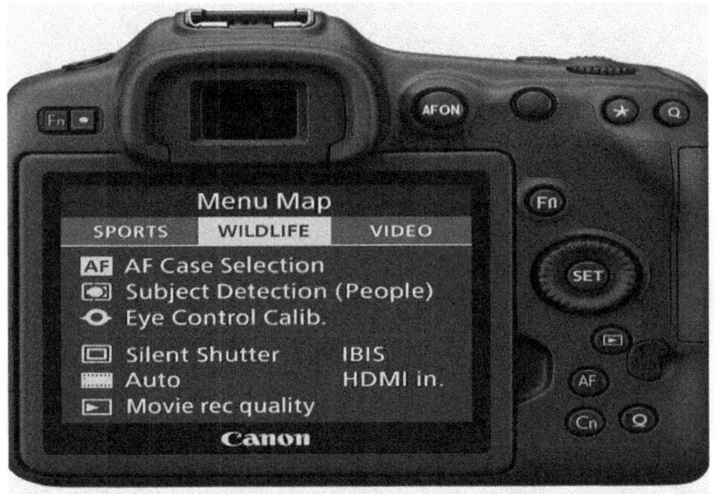

Part II: Autofocus Mastery

Chapter 3

Eye-Controlled Autofocus in Action

A New Way of Seeing

For many photographers, autofocus has always been about hands: selecting a point with a joystick, moving a dial, or trusting the camera to decide. With the EOS R1, Canon reintroduces a system that feels closer to science fiction than photography: Eye-Controlled Autofocus (ECAF).

This isn't just technology—it's a shift in the relationship between photographer and camera. Instead of moving a joystick or selecting a point, your gaze tells the camera where to focus. Done right, it feels like the camera is an extension of your vision itself. But like all powerful tools, it demands patience, practice, and trust.

Training Your Eye for Precision

The first time you enable ECAF, you may be surprised by how responsive—and unforgiving—it is. Your eyes flicker constantly, scanning scenes faster than you realize. The R1 sees those micro-movements and translates them into commands. That means without training, your AF point may seem to dance unpredictably.

To tame this, you need eye discipline. Think of it like developing a golfer's swing or a pianist's touch—small refinements lead to muscle memory.

Calibration is step one.

- Go through the calibration process carefully, under the same lighting you'll shoot in.

- Repeat calibrations for different situations (bright sun, low light, glasses/contacts).

- Save multiple profiles if you wear different eyewear.

Focus your gaze, not just your mind.

- Look directly at the subject, not around it.

- Avoid "darting eyes"—practice holding your gaze steady for at least one full second.

Practice with static subjects first.

- Place an object against a busy background.

- Train yourself to "select with the eyes, confirm with the shutter."

- Don't rush—this isn't about speed yet, it's about accuracy.

With time, you'll notice your eyes learn a kind of photographic discipline: no wasted glances, no stray focus jumps, only intent.

When Eye Control Excels—And When to Fall

Back

Eye-Controlled AF isn't a silver bullet. Like every tool, it shines in some situations and struggles in others. Knowing when to use it—and when to switch—is part of mastery.

Where it excels:

- **Sports:** Locking onto a single player in a chaotic field. Your eyes naturally follow the ball or the athlete; the R1 follows you.

- **Events:** Choosing a face in a crowded room—your glance is faster than navigating menus.

- **Wildlife:** Isolating one bird in a flock or a single animal in tall grass.

Where to be cautious:

- **Extreme low light:** The system can misinterpret eye movement if the scene is dim or your pupils are dilated.

- **Fast panning sequences:** If your eyes scan across multiple players or subjects quickly, the AF point may "skip."

- **Tiny subjects at distance:** For example, a bird against a blue sky may be easier to grab with a traditional AF point or zone method.

The pro's trick is flexibility: start with Eye-Controlled AF, but keep a backup button mapped to instantly switch to another AF mode (like Wide or Single Point). This way, you're never locked into one method.

Field Practice Drills: Trusting Under Pressure

Like any skill, ECAF becomes second nature only through repetition. Here are drills to build confidence:

Drill 1: Static Selection

- Place three objects at varying distances (near, mid, far).

- Practice shifting focus between them only with your eyes, no joystick.

- Confirm focus with half-press of the shutter.

Drill 2: Human Movement

- Ask a friend to walk across the frame.

- Use ECAF to track them, forcing your gaze to stay steady on the subject.

- Repeat with faster movement to build reflexes.

Drill 3: Wildlife Prep

- Go to a park with birds or dogs running off-leash.

- Practice locking on a single moving subject among many.

- This simulates real-world chaos and helps you develop selective eye discipline.

Drill 4: Pressure Simulation

- Time yourself. Give 10 seconds to capture 3–5 sharp images of moving subjects using only ECAF.

- The goal is not perfection—it's building trust that, under stress, your eye + R1 will deliver.

Building Trust

At first, you may not believe ECAF will keep up in critical situations. But as you train, something clicks: you begin to forget the joystick exists. You no longer "select an AF point"—you simply look, and the camera follows. That is the moment of trust.

Under pressure—when the game-winning shot happens, when the eagle dives, when the bride laughs unexpectedly—you won't think about focus at all. You'll be present, your camera tuned to your eyes, capturing exactly what you intend.

This is the promise of Eye-Controlled Autofocus: not replacing skill, but erasing hesitation. It's you, faster, sharper, more connected to the moment than ever before.

STATIC SELECTION

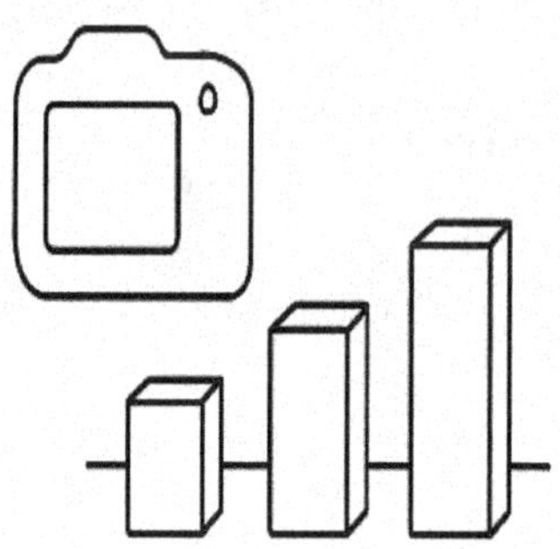

Use eye control to focus
on one of three static obets

HUMAN MOVEMENT

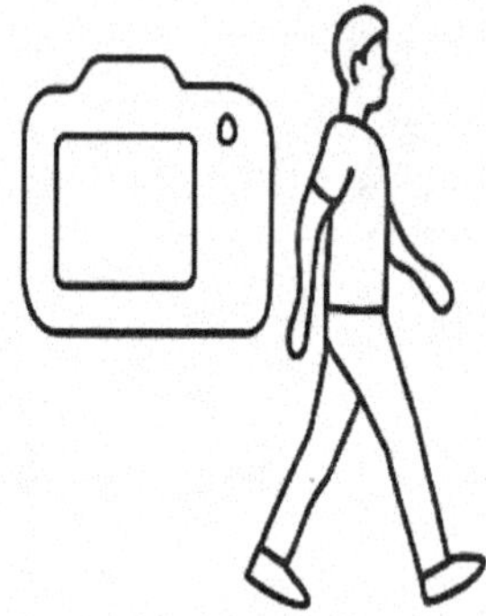

Track a person moving
across the frame
using your eyes

WILDLIFE PREP

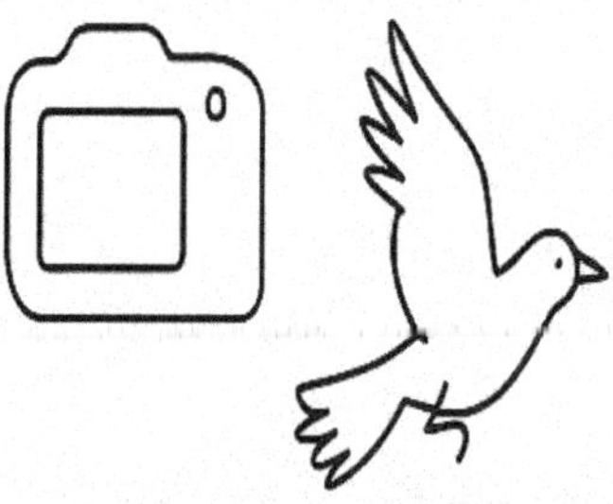

Lock onto a moving subject
in a wildlife setting

PRESSURE SIMULATION

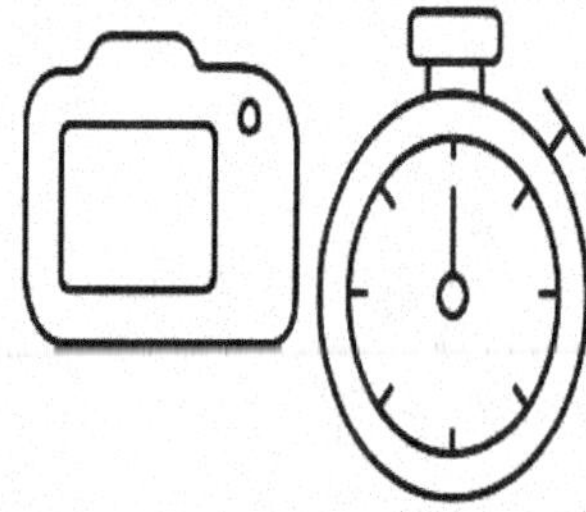

Capture multiple shots
of action in 10 seconds

Chapter 4

AF Cases & Tracking Recipes

Why AF Cases Matter

The Canon EOS R1 inherits Canon's deep autofocus intelligence, building on decades of professional refinement. At its core are the AF Cases—predefined sets of autofocus behaviors designed to anticipate different kinds of subject movement.

Think of AF Cases as behavioral profiles for the camera. Just as an athlete trains differently for sprinting versus long-distance, your R1 tunes its autofocus differently depending on the subject you're tracking. Understanding these cases—and adapting them to real-world scenarios—is what elevates your keeper rate from good to outstanding.

Sports AF Case Breakdown

Sports photography is where milliseconds make or break a shot. The R1's AF Cases are designed to read acceleration, deceleration, direction changes, and erratic motion. Let's break down real sports scenarios:

Indoor Basketball

- **AF Case:** Case 2 (continue to track subjects, ignoring obstacles)
- **Why:** In basketball, players weave in and out, often crossing in front of one another. This case tells the R1 to stick to your chosen player and ignore temporary obstructions like referees or defenders.
- **Recipe:**
  - AF Method: Whole Area Tracking + Eye Control to select your player.
  - Lens: 70–200mm f/2.8 RF for court coverage.

- o Tip: Map the rate button to instantly toggle to Single Point for free throws or isolated plays.

Football (Soccer or American)

- **AF Case:** Case 4 (subjects that accelerate or decelerate quickly)

- **Why:** Players burst forward, stop abruptly, or change direction with the ball. This case allows AF to react aggressively.

- **Recipe:**

  - o AF Method: Zone AF, centered but large enough to cover quick shifts.

  - o Lens: 400mm f/2.8 RF for reach.

  - o Tip: Activate Pre-Shooting Burst—goals happen in split seconds, and pre-buffering gives you the shot just before the kick.

- **AF Case:** Case 3 (instantly focusing on subjects that enter AF point)

- **Why:** Runners, hurdlers, or jumpers enter your frame quickly from a distance. This case prioritizes rapid acquisition.

- **Recipe:**

  - AF Method: Single Point or Expand AF around finish line.

  - Lens: 100–300mm f/2.8 RF for flexibility.

  - Tip: Anticipate; lock AF just before the athlete crosses into range.

Wildlife AF Tracking Recipes

Nature is unpredictable. The R1's subject-detection modes combined with AF Cases give wildlife shooters an edge.

Birds in Flight

- **AF Case:** Case 2 (tracking despite obstructions)
- **Why:** Birds often fly through branches or against complex backgrounds. This case holds focus on your bird even when the scene gets messy.
- **Recipe:**
  - AF Method: Whole Area with Subject Detection set to Animals.
  - Lens: 600mm f/4 RF or 100–500mm RF for flexibility.
  - Tip: Use Eye Control to pick your bird out of a flock instantly.

Mammals in Motion

- **AF Case:** Case 4 (fast acceleration/deceleration)
- **Why:** Deer, lions, or bears may bolt suddenly. Case 4 ensures AF doesn't lag behind bursts of speed.
- **Recipe:**

o   AF Method: Large Zone AF, Eye Control enabled.

o   Lens: 400mm f/2.8 RF.

o   Tip: Keep shutter speed high (1/2000s or faster). Blur ruins wildlife shots more than noise ever will.

Low-Light Predators

- **AF Case:** Case 1 (standard, versatile tracking)

- **Why:** In near-darkness, overly aggressive AF can "hunt." A balanced case works best.

- **Recipe:**

  o   AF Method: Spot AF or Small Zone.

  o   Lens: Fast prime (RF 135mm f/1.8) or telephoto with strong IS.

  o   Tip: Enable "Low Light AF Assist" but be cautious—avoid distracting animals with IR beam.

Event AF Tricks

Events combine unpredictability with critical, once-only moments. Here's where the R1's intelligence shines, if you know how to guide it.

Weddings

- **AF Case:** Case 2 (stay locked despite obstacles)
- **Why:** Guests, veils, or bouquets often obscure the couple briefly.
- **Recipe:**
    - AF Method: Face/Eye Detect with Eye Control.
    - Lens: 24–70mm f/2.8 RF for versatility.
    - Tip: Assign "Instant Eye Switch" to a custom button for bride vs. groom during vows.

Concerts

- **AF Case:** Case 5 (tracking with erratic, zig-zag movement)

- **Why:** Performers move unpredictably across stage with wild lighting.

- **Recipe:**

  - AF Method: Wide Tracking, Eye Control to select singer.

  - Lens: 70–200mm f/2.8 RF.

  - Tip: Use Anti-Flicker and high shutter speed (1/500s) to counter LED stage lights.

Unpredictable Crowds

- **AF Case:** Case 1 (general-purpose) or Case 2 if choosing one subject.

- **Why:** Case 1 is balanced for shifting groups; Case 2 holds onto one person.

- **Recipe:**

  - AF Method: Zone AF, Eye Control to grab key moments (smiles, reactions).

  - Lens: 35mm or 50mm RF prime for intimacy.

o Tip: Keep depth-of-field forgiving (f/2.8–f/4). Crowds are dynamic, and razor-thin DOF risks missed faces.

The Key Takeaway

The R1's AF Cases aren't abstract—they're tools. Once you know which case matches which scenario, you stop worrying about "settings" and start trusting the camera to stay with you.

- Sports: Prioritize aggression and resilience against obstacles.

- Wildlife: Balance persistence with subject detection for unpredictable movement.

- Events: Protect against interruptions and adapt to chaos.

With practice, you'll build your own library of recipes—shortcuts that align with your instincts. That's when autofocus stops being a technical chore and becomes second nature—an invisible ally in the pursuit of unforgettable images.

SPORTS	WILDLIFE	EVENTS

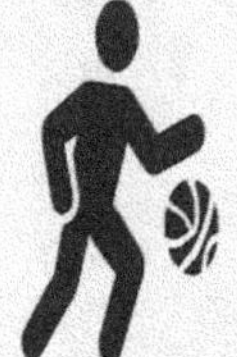

Indoor Basketball

AF Case 2

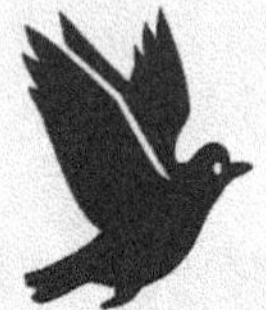

Birds in Flight

AF Case 2

Weddings

AF Case 2

Football

AF Case 4

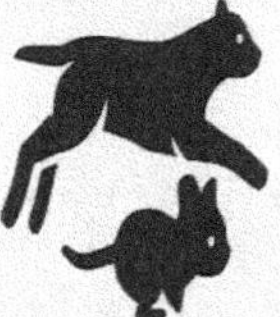

Mammals in Motion

AF Case 4

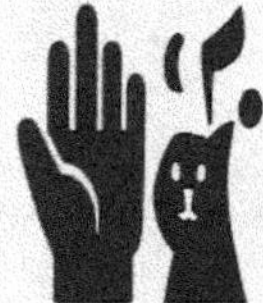

Low-Light Predators

AF Case 1

Track & Field

AF Case 3

Low-Light Predators

AF Case 1

Unpredictable Crowds

AF Case 1

Chapter 5

Low-Light & Challenging Conditions

The Nature of the Challenge

Every camera performs beautifully in broad daylight. It's in the dim corners of an indoor arena, the candlelit glow of a wedding reception, or the chaotic rainbow of a concert stage where a camera truly proves its worth. These are the conditions that push the EOS R1's autofocus system and exposure reliability to their limits—and where knowing how to configure your gear can mean the difference between a blurry miss and a career-defining shot.

The R1 has been designed for pros who live in these environments: journalists filing from dimly lit press briefings, wildlife photographers waiting at dusk, event shooters navigating unpredictable backlighting. In this chapter, we'll examine how to push the autofocus system in low light, pair lenses with AF strategies for maximum reliability, and overcome the technical traps of flicker, backlight, and LED lighting.

Pushing AF to the Limits in Dim Venues and Arenas

Canon engineered the R1 with autofocus sensitivity that can lock onto subjects down to very low light levels. But performance in practice depends on technique as much as technology.

Key approaches:

- Use larger AF zones in low light. In dim scenes, tiny AF points can struggle to acquire contrast. Switch to Zone AF or Whole Area Tracking with Eye Detection enabled—it gives the system more to work with.

- Prioritize subject detection. Even in near-darkness, the R1's Deep Learning AF can identify eyes and faces. Keep "Detect People" or "Detect Animals" active when it matters most.

- Leverage Eye-Control AF cautiously. Eye Control can still be effective in low light, but if your gaze feels jittery or if the camera hesitates, don't be afraid to fall back on Wide AF or Single Point.

- Boost reliability with exposure aids. Enable the electronic viewfinder's gain-up mode—even when your eyes can't see details, the EVF amplifies light to help you frame and focus.

In short: don't fight the system—give it more information, and it will reward you with sharp focus even in venues that test your vision.

Pairing Lenses with AF Settings for Reliability

The R1 is only as strong as the lens you mount on it. In low light, aperture speed and stabilization play a crucial role in AF performance.

Fast Primes for Precision

- Lenses like the RF 50mm f/1.2L or RF 85mm f/1.2L give autofocus the maximum amount of light. This speeds up subject recognition and reduces hunting in dim spaces.

- Best for: weddings, portraits, and creative low-light work where shallow depth of field is an advantage.

Telephoto Powerhouses

- In arenas, you may lean on longer lenses like the RF 70–200mm f/2.8L or RF 400mm f/2.8L. Their wide apertures and Canon's dual-pixel AF system keep focus locked even when athletes are under patchy floodlights.

- Best for: indoor sports, large events, and stage coverage.

Stabilized Zooms for Flexibility

- The RF 24–70mm f/2.8L and RF 100–500mm f/4.5–7.1L (with strong IS) can handle more versatile scenarios. Even though the latter isn't as fast, the R1's IBIS + lens IS pairing makes it surprisingly capable for wildlife at dawn or dusk.

- Best for: travel, dynamic events, and wildlife when mobility matters more than pure aperture speed.

AF Settings that Complement Lenses

- For fast primes: use Single Point AF or Small Zone AF for accuracy.

- For telephotos: pair with Case 4 (acceleration/deceleration) to keep up with fast-moving subjects.

- For stabilized zooms: rely on Whole Area Tracking when subjects may appear unpredictably.

The takeaway: match the AF method to the lens's strengths. Don't force a long telephoto into tiny AF points or expect a slow zoom to track erratic subjects in near-darkness without compromise.

Handling Flicker, Backlight & LED Lighting

Challenges

Low light is only half the battle. Artificial lighting introduces its own hazards: flicker, strange color shifts, and brutal backlighting that can confuse both exposure and AF.

Flicker in Arenas & Gyms

- Fluorescent and LED lights often pulse faster than your eye can detect. The result: uneven exposures or banding in images.

- Solution: Enable the R1's Anti-Flicker Shooting mode. The camera times the shutter to the peak of the light cycle, delivering consistent exposure.

- Pro Tip: In critical moments, use Electronic 1st Curtain Shutter instead of fully electronic to reduce rolling band artifacts.

Backlight at Events

- Brides under arched windows, keynote speakers on spotlighted stages, wildlife silhouetted at sunset—all of these test exposure metering.

- Solution: Switch to Spot Metering tied to AF point. This ensures your subject is exposed correctly, not the glowing background.

- Pro Tip: Dial in +1 EV exposure compensation when backlit faces look too shadowed.

LED Stage Lights at Concerts

- Saturated blues, purples, and rapid shifts can confuse AF and ruin skin tones.

- Solution: Lock white balance to a preset (Tungsten or Daylight) instead of Auto, to avoid color-hunting mid-performance.

- Pro Tip: Shoot in RAW for maximum recovery flexibility—LED lighting is unpredictable, and RAW preserves the range you need to fix it later.

The Professional Edge

Low light and challenging environments are the crucible of professional photography. Anyone can capture sharp images at noon; it's in the dim, difficult, unpredictable moments where skill, preparation, and the right tools separate professionals from amateurs.

The Canon EOS R1 is built for these crucibles. Its autofocus system, when tuned correctly, sees deeper into shadows than your eyes. Its lenses and stabilization systems make handheld work possible where tripods are banned. Its anti-flicker and exposure tools tame the chaos of artificial light.

Mastering these conditions isn't about fighting limitations—it's about embracing them as part of the craft. The best images are often the hardest won, and with the R1 properly configured, you'll be ready to create them.

Low-Lilght & Challenging Conditions

Dim Venues

- Use zone AF
- Enable subject detect
- Gain-up MF

Lens Pairings

- Fast primes
- Telephotos
- Stabilized zooms

Lighting Challenges

- Anti-flicker
- Spot metering
- Lock white balance

Part III: Exposure, Speed & Control

Chapter 6

Pre-Shooting Burst & Speed Tactics

Why Speed Matters

In sports and wildlife photography, milliseconds are everything. The difference between a bird captured mid-wingbeat or mid-blink, between a soccer ball on the player's foot or just after it leaves, is often a fraction of a second. The Canon EOS R1's Pre-Shooting Burst feature is designed for those fractions—it allows you to capture frames before you actually press the shutter fully.

Combined with blistering frame rates and a deep buffer, the R1 transforms how you approach fast action. But to harness this technology, you need to understand how to configure it, how to balance frame rates against file management, and how to refine your timing through field practice.

How to Set and Use Pre-Shooting Burst

What it does: Pre-Shooting Burst continuously buffers frames as you half-press the shutter. When you press fully, it saves not only the frames after your press, but also those from just before—usually up to 0.5 seconds earlier.

This means you can capture the basketball leaving a player's fingertips, the eagle's talons striking water, or a sprinter's explosive first stride—even if your own reflexes were a hair late.

How to set it up:

1. Navigate to Drive Mode in the Shooting Menu.

2. Select Electronic Shutter: H+ (High-Speed).

3. Enable Pre-Shooting Burst and choose your desired pre-buffer duration (commonly 0.5 sec).

4. Practice: half-press to start buffering, then fully press when action unfolds.

Pro Tip: Keep your finger lightly half-pressed when anticipating

action. Train your muscle memory not to relax too soon—if you lift

yc

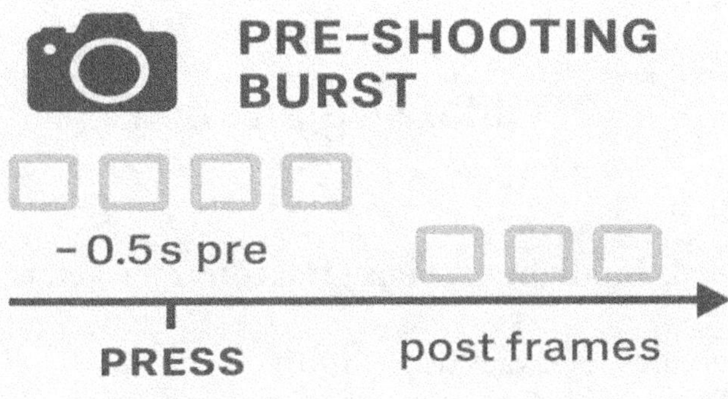

Sports Applications

- Basketball: When you know a dunk or layup is coming, half-press as the player drives, then fire just before they jump. The pre-buffer ensures you'll have the release moment.

- Soccer/Football: Anticipate free kicks or penalty shots. The instant before contact is notoriously hard to time—pre-burst covers it.

- Track & Field: Use at the starting line. Even if your reaction lags behind the starter's gun, the R1 will capture the initial stride.

Wildlife Applications

- **Birds in Flight:** Anticipate takeoff from a branch. Pre-burst captures the exact wing lift-off.

- **Predatory Strikes:** Whether it's a heron spearing fish or a lion lunging, the pre-buffer preserves the strike, not just the aftermath.

- **Elusive Behavior:** Many animals flick ears, tails, or wings quickly. Pre-shooting burst ensures you don't miss subtle gestures that make a photo feel alive.

Balancing Frame Rate with Buffer & Card

Choices

The R1 is capable of staggering frame rates, but speed without strategy leads to clogged buffers, filled cards, and wasted editing time. To work like a pro, you must balance.

Frame Rates to Consider:

- 30 fps: Maximum speed, best for moments that cannot be missed (sprinter starts, bird takeoff).

- 20 fps: Balanced for continuous action where you'll track a subject for a longer sequence (soccer matches, concerts).

- 15 fps or lower: Practical for extended coverage where card space matters (ceremonies, slower wildlife).

Buffer Behavior:

- With top-end CFexpress Type B cards, the R1 can sustain long bursts before slowing.

- With slower or smaller cards, the buffer fills faster, forcing the camera to pause while writing.

Card Recommendations:

- Sports Pros: At least 512GB CFexpress cards rated for sustained 1400–1600 MB/s write speed.

- Wildlife Pros: Carry multiple smaller cards (256GB) rather than one giant card, to reduce risk of total loss if a card fails.

- Events: Dual-card setup with CFexpress for RAW + SD for JPEG backups.

Pro Tip: Know your buffer limits. Test your camera: hold down the shutter at 30 fps until it slows. Count the seconds. This tells you exactly how long you can rely on uninterrupted high-speed coverage in real work.

Lessons from Field-Tested Sequences

Over time, professionals learn that speed isn't just about holding down the shutter—it's about knowing when to unleash it.

- The Anticipation Shot: In basketball, the moment a player's shoulders dip before a jump shot signals what's coming. Pre-burst and a short controlled sequence catch the release without filling cards with dribbles.

- The Patience Rule: In wildlife, don't fire constantly as a bird perches. Wait, half-press to buffer, then full-press when it stirs. You'll have the takeoff sequence without 600 wasted frames.

- Controlled Chaos: In events, musicians and performers move unpredictably. Instead of maxing out frame rate all night, save 30 fps bursts for signature moves (leaps, applause moments). Run lower fps for the rest to preserve buffer and sanity.

What these lessons teach: Speed is a tool, not a crutch. The most successful shooters use pre-burst and high fps sparingly but strategically. The R1's intelligence covers your human reflexes, but your instincts—reading the game, the animal, or the stage—remain irreplaceable.

The Professional Edge

The EOS R1 isn't about brute force. It's about using speed smartly. Pre-Shooting Burst covers human reaction lag; frame-rate control balances buffer and workflow; field-tested anticipation turns randomness into reliability.

When mastered, these tactics give you not just more photos, but the right photos—the decisive frames that define your story.

How to Set and Use Pre-Shooting Burst for Sports/Wildlife

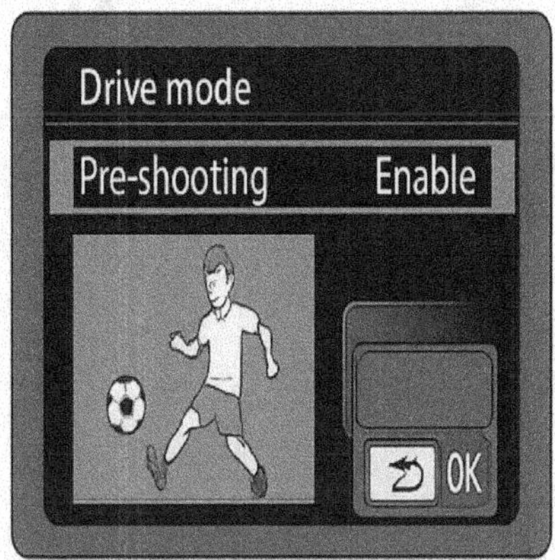

Balancing Frame Rate with Buffer and Card Choices

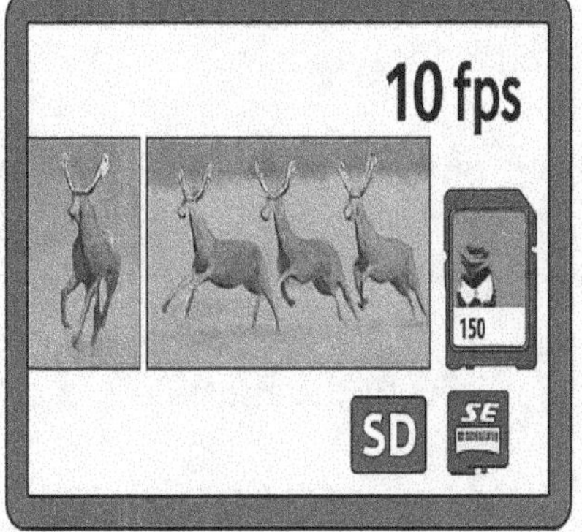

Lessons from Field-Tested Sequences

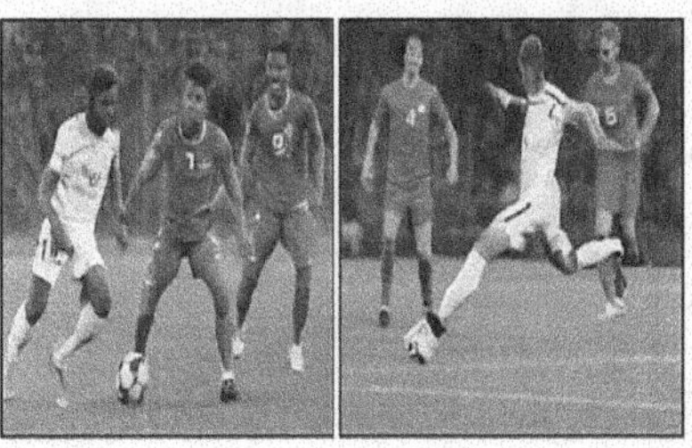

Chapter 7

Exposure & Metering Blueprints

The Art of Fast Exposure

Exposure control is the heart of every photograph. In calm, controlled conditions, you can experiment leisurely. But in fast-changing environments—athletes under uneven stadium lights, wildlife bursting from shadow into sunlight, performers moving from spotlight to darkness—you don't get time to deliberate. You need blueprints: reliable strategies that make exposure decisions quick, accurate, and instinctive.

The Canon EOS R1 gives you professional tools like exposure compensation, live histograms, zebras, and advanced ISO management. This chapter shows how to weave them together into a system you can trust in the field.

Exposure Compensation Strategies for Fast-Changing Action

When light shifts rapidly, dialing in manual exposure for every scene is impossible. Exposure compensation (EC) becomes your lifeline.

Key strategies:

1. For Backlit Subjects

    o Problem: Athletes or subjects silhouetted against bright skies or stadium lights.

    o Solution: Dial in +1 EV to +1.7 EV EC to lift your subject out of shadow.

    o Pro Tip: Tie EC to a rear dial for instant thumb adjustment—no menu diving.

2. For Spotlit Performers or Faces

    o Problem: A singer under a spotlight looks blown out while the background goes black.

o Solution: –0.3 to –1 EV EC preserves skin tones, protecting highlights.

o Pro Tip: Use Highlight Tone Priority in-camera when detail in faces is critical.

3. For Erratic Lighting (Clouds, Arenas, Concerts)

o Problem: Light intensity changes mid-action.

o Solution: Start at 0 EC and adjust in small increments (+/–0.3 EV). Overcompensating creates more problems than it solves.

o Pro Tip: Practice "exposure riding"—gently feathering EC on the dial as light changes, without taking your eye from the viewfinder.

In all cases, the goal is consistency across the sequence. A keeper set of 20 frames with uniform exposure is more valuable than 200 frames with wild fluctuations.

Zebra Patterns, Histograms & Highlight

Warnings in the Field

The R1 gives you three professional exposure monitors: zebras, histograms, and highlight warnings. Each has its role.

Zebra Patterns

- Best for: Video or live-action where exposure must be judged in real time.

- Set two levels: e.g., 70% for skin tones, 95% for clipping highlights.

- Use them to prevent overexposure on faces in concerts, weddings, or press events.

Histograms

- Best for: Still images where precision matters.
- Rely on the RGB histogram (not just luminance). A spike on the red channel during a concert means skin tones may be blown even if the overall image looks fine.

- Check histograms during breaks in action; don't overanalyze mid-play.

Highlight Warnings ("Blinkies")

- Best for: Quick field checks between bursts.

- After a sequence, review your shots. If critical highlights blink, adjust EC or ISO before the next sequence.

Field Blueprint:

- Use zebras for continuous monitoring.

- Use histograms to double-check exposure during pauses.

- Use blinkies as a quick safety check before moving on.

This layered approach gives you both real-time assurance and post-shot confirmation.

Manual vs. Auto ISO When Seconds Count

ISO is often overlooked, but it's your hidden ally in fast action. Choosing between manual ISO and Auto ISO depends on whether consistency or adaptability matters most.

Manual ISO

- Best for: Controlled conditions (consistent lighting across the field, press conference indoors, wildlife in steady dawn light).

- Benefits: Predictable results, identical exposures frame to frame.

- Blueprint: Pair Manual ISO with Manual Exposure when you cannot risk fluctuations.

Auto ISO

- Best for: Dynamic conditions (clouds passing over, concerts with flashing lights, sports in mixed arena lighting).

- Benefits: Camera adjusts ISO instantly to preserve shutter speed/aperture priorities.

- Blueprint:

  - Set ISO Range (e.g., 100–12,800) to prevent overreach.

  - Lock in shutter speed and aperture critical to your scene.

  - Let ISO absorb the variability.

Pro Hybrid Strategy

- Use Auto ISO + Exposure Compensation together.

- Example: Shooting soccer under floodlights: lock shutter at 1/2000s, aperture at f/2.8, ISO Auto capped at 12,800. Then use EC dial to fine-tune as players move between bright and shadowed areas.

- This keeps action frozen while exposure adapts without hesitation.

Lessons from the Field

- **At a basketball game indoors:** Shooting manual ISO at 3200 worked until a dramatic spotlight intro scene. Switching to Auto ISO + EC meant no frames were lost when the light changed.

- **At a wedding ceremony:** Manual ISO kept exposures consistent across 200 shots under steady indoor lighting, saving hours in post-production.

- **On safari:** A lion emerging from shade into sunlight proved why Auto ISO with capped max was invaluable—the exposure stayed balanced without blown highlights or crushed shadows.

The Professional Edge

Exposure mastery is not about memorizing settings—it's about reading the scene and applying the right blueprint instantly.

- Use EC like a steering wheel to correct quickly in dynamic action.

- Rely on zebras and histograms as your navigational instruments.

- Choose Auto ISO when speed rules, Manual ISO when consistency is king.

When you combine these tools into muscle memory, exposure stops being a distraction. It becomes seamless, letting you focus on what matters most: the story unfolding in front of your lens.

Exposure & Metering Blueprints

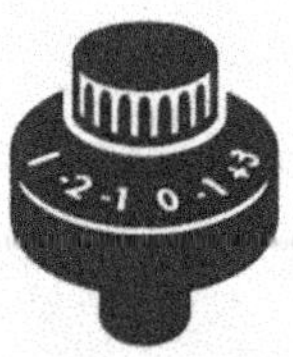

Exposure Compensation

for fast-changing action

Zebra Patterns, Histograms

and highlight warnings

Manual vs. Auto ISO

when seconds count

Part IV: Real-World Shooting Recipes

Chapter 8

Sports Masterclass

When you step into the arena, whether it's the dim hum of a basketball gym, the sweeping chaos of a football stadium, or the merciless pace of track and field, the Canon EOS R1 stops being just a tool and becomes a tactical partner. This chapter isn't theory—it's the collected muscle memory of field-tested setups, the kind that let you react faster than instinct. The R1's engineering makes it possible, but your preparation makes it real.

Setup Maps for Different Sports

Indoor Sports (Basketball, Volleyball, Hockey)

Indoor arenas pose three challenges at once: dim light, unpredictable flicker, and players who move with split-second bursts. Here's how to configure the R1 for dominance indoors:

- AF Setup:

    o   AF Case 2 with Eye-Control engaged.

    o   Zone AF (expanded) for chaotic scenes under the hoop.

    o   Servo AF with people detection prioritized.

- Drive Mode:

    o   20–30 fps burst, moderated by buffer to avoid choking mid-play.

    o   Pre-shooting burst on, so you catch the dunk *before* the hand hits rim.

- Exposure & Flicker Control:

    o   Enable anti-flicker shooting for LED lights.

    o   Shutter speed locked at 1/1000 minimum; raise ISO as needed.

    o   Use custom WB set to arena lights to avoid green shifts.

This setup lets you grab the fast break without clipping highlights from overhead lights.

Outdoor Field Sports (Football, Soccer, Rugby, Track & Field)

Outdoors brings light, but also speed across distance—athletes often moving from shadow to bright sun in a single stride.

- AF Setup:
    - AF Case 4 for accelerating/decelerating subjects.
    - Eye-Control AF for isolating players in a scrum or sprint.
    - For track and field, set AF tracking sensitivity lower to avoid losing the sprinter among lane markers.
- Drive Mode:
    - 20–30 fps continuous with large buffer cards (CFexpress B recommended).
    - Assign "rate" button to instantly flag keepers during bursts.
- Exposure & Metering:

- o Evaluative metering for daylight; manual exposure locked in changing stadium sun.

- o Auto ISO capped to protect shadows but avoid blowing highlights.

Here, the R1's deep buffer lets you hold the shutter through an entire sprint without missing the finish line celebration.

Extreme Action (Motocross, Skiing, Skateboarding)

For sports with unpredictable trajectories, the key is predictive AF and durability under punishing environments.

- AF Setup:

  - o AF Case 5 for erratic subjects.

  - o Wide AF zones with eye/helmet detection active.

  - o Subject tracking set to "responsive" for jumps and spins.

- Drive Mode:

  - o Push 30 fps for aerial tricks.

- o Pre-shooting burst critical for takeoff moments.

- Exposure & Support:

  - o Shutter priority at 1/2000 or faster for airborne freezes.

  - o Protective filters and weather sealing engaged— dust, snow, and mud test every seam.

These setups ensure the rider's expression mid-air is tack sharp, even with dirt flying at your lens.

Lens Pairing Strategies by Sport

Sports are unforgiving if you bring the wrong glass. The R1 rewards preparation with pro-grade consistency:

- Indoor Sports: Fast primes are king. A 70–200mm f/2.8 is the universal workhorse, but consider 135mm f/1.8 for shallow depth isolation in cramped courts.

- Outdoor Field Sports: The 400mm f/2.8 is legendary, but a 200–400mm f/4 with built-in 1.4x offers versatility without losing AF performance. On a budget, the 100–500mm RF delivers reach with stabilization.

- Extreme Sports: Wide zooms like 15–35mm f/2.8 for immersive "close-proximity" shots. Pair with a 24–70mm f/2.8 for run-and-gun flexibility.

Each lens pairing should be tied to your shooting position. Courtside vs. sideline vs. press box can mean swapping reach for responsiveness.

Heat Management During Long 4K/6K Coverage

Shooting extended sports coverage in 4K or 6K demands attention not just to players, but to your camera's thermals:

1. Pre-Event Prep:

   o Keep the camera shaded before start; avoid powering it on too early.

    o   Use high-capacity batteries to reduce swap-induced heat spikes.

2. During Coverage:

    o   Record in segments instead of one marathon clip; let the sensor breathe.

    o   Offload files quickly to avoid buffer holding excess heat.

3. Practical Tactics:

    o   Use a monopod to shift physical heat load off your body.

    o   Carry silica packs for condensation control if transitioning from warm to cold venues.

Canon engineered the R1 with advanced heat sinks, but physics always wins in the long haul—your job is to extend uptime strategically.

Closing Field Note

Every sport punishes hesitation. With the EOS R1, your edge comes not from luck, but from deliberate mastery of its speed-driven DNA. If you set your rigs with these recipes, the camera disappears in your hands—and all that's left is the story of motion, sweat, and victory.

Setup Maps for Different Sports

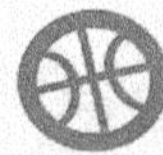 Indoor Sports

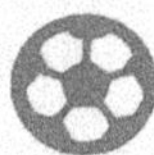 Outdoor Field Sports

 Extreme Action

Lens Pairing Strategies by Sport

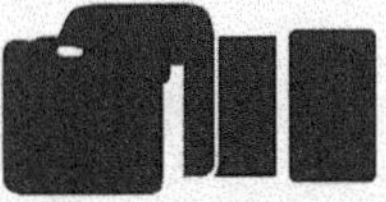

Heat Management During Long 4K/6K Coverage

Chapter 9

Wildlife Masterclass

Wildlife photography isn't just about the gear—it's about predicting behavior, adapting to unpredictable light, and having a camera setup that reacts faster than you can think. The Canon EOS R1 is uniquely suited for this because of its autofocus intelligence, rugged stamina, and pre-shooting burst features. But using it effectively in the field, whether for birds slicing the sky or mammals prowling in twilight, requires deliberate setups and habits.

Birds in Flight – Step-by-Step AF Setup

Photographing birds in flight is a brutal test for any autofocus system. Their erratic paths, sudden dives, and fast wingbeats make locking focus a challenge. Here's how to turn the R1 into a bird-tracking machine:

1. **AF Area Selection – Flexible Zone AF:**

Choose a small-to-medium AF zone rather than the entire frame. Too large a zone risks locking onto background elements like trees or clouds. A flexible zone lets the EOS R1's intelligent subject detection find and cling to the bird's head or body.

2. **Subject Tracking – Animal Priority Enabled:**

Activate Animal Subject Detection, which now includes bird-specific algorithms. The camera will prioritize the head and eyes, even if the wings flap across the frame.

3. **Servo AF Case – Case 2 (Continue Tracking, Ignore Obstacles):**

This ensures the camera won't dump focus if a wing crosses over the head or if the bird briefly passes behind branches.

4. **Frame Rate – 30fps Pre-Shooting Burst:**

Use bursts to capture wing cycles at the perfect point of extension. With pre-shooting enabled, you can grab the decisive moment even if your reflex was late.

5. **Stabilization Mode – IS Mode 2:**

For panning shots of birds in motion, Mode 2 disables stabilization on the horizontal axis, keeping your pans smooth without fighting the IS system.

Long-Lens Stabilization Tricks

A 400mm, 600mm, or 800mm lens unlocks reach but magnifies every micro-vibration. Even on a pro body like the R1, stabilization technique matters as much as the lens choice.

- **Tripod + Gimbal:** For long waits in blinds or wetlands, a gimbal head balances the lens so that movement feels weightless. This setup allows tracking a bird's erratic flight without fighting gravity.

- **Monopod Technique:** In places where a tripod is impractical, use a monopod with a fluid tilt head. Angle it slightly forward to absorb recoil when you pan upward.

- **Handholding Big Glass:** If handheld, keep elbows tucked into your torso, support the lens barrel with your left hand, and press the viewfinder firmly against your eyebrow to create a third point of contact.

- **IBIS + Lens IS Sync:** Modern Canon telephotos sync with in-body stabilization, delivering up to 7–8 stops of shake correction. But beware: turn IS *off* when mounted on a tripod, otherwise micro-adjustments may introduce blur.

Managing Battery Life in Remote Shoots

When you're hours into a trek or camping far from power, the EOS R1's performance demands must be balanced with conservation tactics.

- **Use LP-E19 Batteries (Pro Grade):** The R1 is built for these high-capacity packs. Carry at least two spares for a full day of wildlife work, especially if shooting bursts.

- **Conserve in Standby:** Enable "Eco Mode" to reduce EVF refresh when idle. It won't affect your shooting readiness, but can extend runtime by 20–30%.

- **Disable Unnecessary Features:** GPS, Wi-Fi, and Bluetooth drain silently in the background. Turn them off unless you're transferring files in the field.

- **External USB-C Power Banks:** For multi-day expeditions, use a PD-compatible power bank to top up batteries without needing AC power.

- **Buffer Discipline:** Shooting continuous 30fps bursts burns through batteries faster. Use shorter, purposeful bursts instead of holding down the shutter.

Field Wisdom – The Wildlife Mindset

Wildlife photography rewards patience as much as technical mastery. The R1 can track a falcon through a dive or isolate the eye of a leopard in shadows, but it's only as effective as your fieldcraft. Learn to anticipate flight paths, study animal behavior, and keep your setups consistent so that when the moment comes, muscle memory takes over.

The combination of Canon's flagship autofocus, long-lens discipline, and careful power management transforms the EOS R1 into a wildlife specialist. The machine is capable—your job is to give it the time, discipline, and field strategy to make it shine.

WILDLIFE MASTERCLASS

BIRDS IN FLIGHT AF SETUP	LONG-LENS STABILIZATION TRICKS	MANAGING BATTERY LIFE IN REMOTE SHOOTS
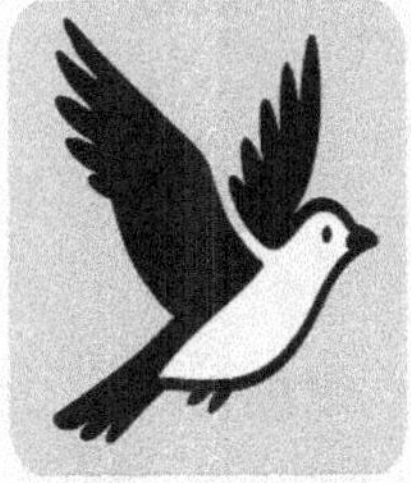	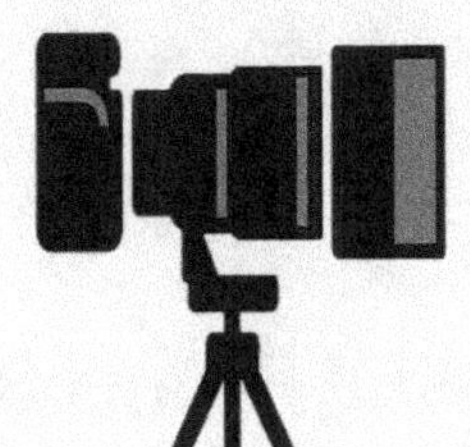	
. AF Area: Flexible Zone AF . Subject Tracking: Animal Priority Enabled . Servo AF Case: Case 2 . Frame Rate: 30fps Pre-Shooting Burst	. Tripod + Gimbal . Monopod Technique . Handholding Big Glass . IBIS + Lens IS Sync	. Use LP-E19 Batteries . Conserve in Standby . Disable Unnecessay Features . External USB-C Power Banks

Chapter 10

Event & Documentary Masterclass

Event and documentary photography are unforgiving arenas. Unlike sports or wildlife, where the action follows predictable rhythms, weddings, concerts, and frontline documentary work often collide with chaos, emotion, and lighting conditions that change in the blink of an eye. The EOS R1 is built to thrive in this pressure—if you know how to configure it. This chapter provides blueprint-level guidance on setups for weddings, live performances, and journalistic coverage where you often get just one shot at history.

Weddings: Fast AF Swaps Between Subjects

and Groups

A wedding day is a test of reflexes. One moment you're isolating the bride's tearful expression, the next you're capturing a full family portrait where everyone needs to be in focus.

- AF Mode Shifts:

  Assign a custom button to instantly toggle between Eye Detection AF (for singles) and Zone AF (for groups). This saves you the frustration of diving into menus mid-ceremony.

- Depth-of-Field Strategy:

  For individuals, wide apertures (f/1.2–f/2.8) create the cinematic blur couples love. For groups, stop down to f/4–f/5.6 to keep multiple faces sharp while letting background fall away.

- Silent Shutter Etiquette:

  The R1's electronic shutter allows you to disappear into the ceremony. Silence ensures you never ruin the vows with mechanical clicks.

- Backup Mentality:

Always dual-record to both card slots. Nothing will test your reputation faster than losing images from a once-in-a-lifetime event.

Concerts: Wrestling With LED & Stage Lighting

Concert halls and festivals challenge even seasoned pros. LED lights pulse at invisible frequencies, stage lights wash out faces, and the action rarely pauses.

- Anti-Flicker Settings:

Enable Anti-Flicker Shooting and set high-frequency flicker detection for LED-heavy venues. This reduces color banding that can wreck an otherwise perfect frame.

- Metering Mode Choices:

  Use Spot Metering to lock exposure on the performer's face, not the background haze. Tie spot metering to the AF point so exposure follows your subject.

- Custom White Balance Banks:

  Pre-save several Kelvin values (e.g., 2800K for tungsten wash, 4000K for LED, 5600K for daylight spill). This allows instant correction as lighting shifts.

- ISO Strategy:

  Embrace Auto ISO but set a max value you trust (e.g., 12,800). Pair it with exposure compensation (+0.3 to +0.7) to preserve shadow detail against harsh spotlights.

News & Documentary: Reliability Above All

In documentary or news coverage, you don't control the stage—you react to it. From protests to disaster zones, your EOS R1 must behave like an extension of your instincts.

- One-Chance Settings:

  Use Shutter Priority (Tv) with safety shift enabled. Lock in the minimum speed to freeze action (1/500s or faster) and let aperture/ISO float. This ensures sharp captures under unpredictable lighting.

- AF for Chaos:

  Case 2 or Case 4 AF tracking modes handle subjects moving erratically. Tie AF-ON to back-button focus so you can disengage instantly if the camera latches onto the wrong subject.

- Redundancy Strategy:

  Dual card recording is non-negotiable. Add auto file transfer via the R1's network options if time-critical delivery is part of your workflow.

- Ergonomics Under Pressure:

  Configure the camera so every essential—shutter, ISO, AF point control, white balance—is a button press away. In

frontline work, seconds spent digging through menus are
seconds lost forever.

Final Word

Event and documentary photography hinge less on artistic freedom
and more on consistency. Couples, performers, and audiences don't
wait for you to adjust your camera. The EOS R1 provides the
horsepower, but it's your discipline in customization that allows it
to become invisible—an extension of your presence rather than a
distraction. Whether you're capturing a fleeting kiss, a guitar solo in
strobes, or a protester's raised fist, these setups turn moments into
proof, story, and memory.

EVENT & DOCUMENTARY MASTERCLASS

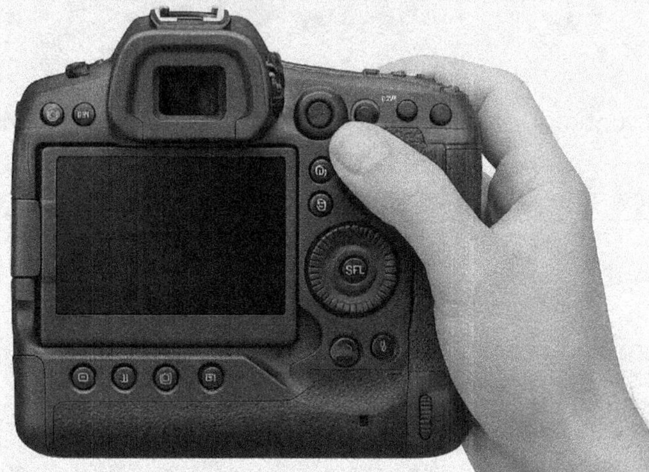

Weddings

Fast AF swaps between single subject and group portraits

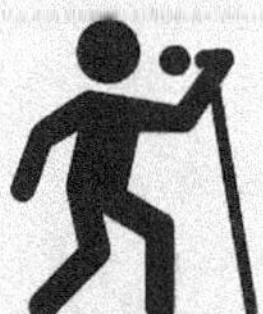

Concerts

Working under LED and fast-changing stage lights

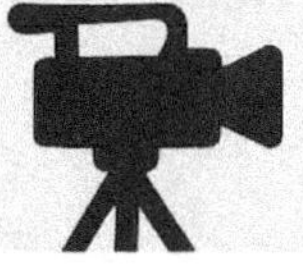

News/Documentary

Reliability setups for one-chance moments

Chapter 11

Pro Video with the R1

6K RAW vs. 4K120p: When and Why | Cooling, Codecs & Card Workflow | Hybrid Rig Builds

The Canon EOS R1 isn't only a stills powerhouse—it's a genuine cinema-class tool designed to meet the demands of professional filmmakers and hybrid shooters. Where older Canon hybrids always seemed to carry a "bias" toward still photography, the R1 feels balanced, offering uncompromising speed for stills while introducing robust video modes that rival dedicated cinema cameras. To use it effectively, though, you need to understand its choices: resolution versus frame rate, compression versus RAW, cooling considerations, and how to rig the body for professional reliability.

6K RAW vs. 4K120p – When and Why

The R1's video muscle centers on two crown jewels: 6K RAW capture and 4K at up to 120p.

- 6K RAW (Full Sensor Readout)

  Shooting 6K RAW gives you unparalleled flexibility in post-production. You capture a 12-bit file with massive latitude for grading, white balance correction, and exposure rescue. It's the mode to use when you're delivering cinematic projects, need to crop or reframe in editing, or want future-proof archival quality. The trade-off? Gigantic file sizes and heavy demands on cards and editing machines. Use 6K RAW when quality is paramount and you control your workflow (commercial shoots, indie films, documentaries where lighting changes fast).

- 4K120p (High Frame Rate)

  If your goal is fluid slow motion for sports highlights, wildlife behavior, or cinematic B-roll, 4K120p is your choice. At 10-bit 4:2:2, it balances quality with practicality. You lose the RAW flexibility but gain manageable file sizes, more shooting time on a card, and fewer overheating risks. Think live event reels, wedding slow-mo entrances, or wildlife wingbeats frozen in smooth detail.

Pro Tip: Many shooters adopt a hybrid workflow—capture key hero shots in 6K RAW, then switch to 4K120p for slow motion inserts. This saves space while keeping the high-end look where it matters most.

Cooling, Codecs, and Card Workflow Explained

Cooling Considerations

High-resolution, high-frame-rate video means heat. The R1 integrates advanced heat dispersion, but long 6K or 4K120p sessions can still push the limits. Smart operators manage this by:

- Shooting in bursts rather than rolling endlessly.

- Using external recorders for certain codecs to reduce internal strain.

- Giving the body short breaks during interviews or concerts.

Codecs & Compression

Canon provides three main levels of video compression:

1. RAW – Highest quality, largest files, ultimate grading control.

2. ALL-I – Intraframe compression, better for editing, larger than IPB but smoother to cut.

3. IPB – Long-GOP compression, smaller files, efficient for run-and-gun shooters, but harder on editing systems.

Card Workflow

The R1's dual CFexpress Type B slots are designed for redundancy and high throughput. Recommendations:

- For 6K RAW, always use matched CFexpress cards rated at the highest sustained write speeds—anything less will result in dropped frames or outright failure.

- For 4K120p IPB/ALL-I, a pro-level CFexpress card still matters, but you can record longer and more reliably without hitting limits.

- Always format in-camera before major shoots, and cycle cards systematically to avoid accidental overwrite.

Pro Workflow: Offload cards after each shooting block, using dual external SSDs (primary + backup). Label your card sets and rotate—this is how professionals avoid workflow disasters.

Hybrid Rig Builds – Tripod, Gimbal, Handheld

The EOS R1 may be compact compared to cinema rigs, but it needs smart support when shooting video:

- Tripod Rig

  For interviews, locked-off shots, or controlled environments, mount the R1 on a sturdy fluid-head tripod. Add-ons: external monitor, shotgun mic, and optional external recorder (Atomos or Blackmagic) for ProRes RAW or cleaner workflows.

- Gimbal Rig

For weddings, real estate, music videos, or sports walk-ins, the R1 shines on a gimbal. Pair it with mid-range RF lenses (24-70mm f/2.8 or 35mm f/1.8) for balanced weight. Always pre-balance with batteries and mic attached to avoid re-tuning mid-shoot.

- Handheld Rig

For documentaries or news capture, agility wins. Use a cage with top handle and minimal accessories—keep weight down for long hours. Rely on Canon's IBIS + lens IS combo for steady handheld work. Add a wireless lav kit or small shotgun for quick audio without bulk.

Field Notes – What Pros Do Differently

- Sports shooters often switch to 4K60p ALL-I for reliability—easier on cards and heat than 120p.

- Wildlife filmmakers combine 6K RAW for feature sequences with 4K IPB for long-roll hides.

- Wedding videographers lean on ALL-I 4K24p for main coverage and drop into 4K120p only for highlight reels.

- Documentarians prize redundancy: dual card recording is non-negotiable, even at the expense of file length.

Key Takeaway: The Canon EOS R1 isn't just a stills legend—it's a true hybrid cinema machine. By mastering the balance of resolution, frame rate, cooling, and workflow, you unlock a system that adapts to sports highlights, weddings, wildlife, and breaking news.

Pro Video with the R1

6K RAW vs. 4K120p: When and Why

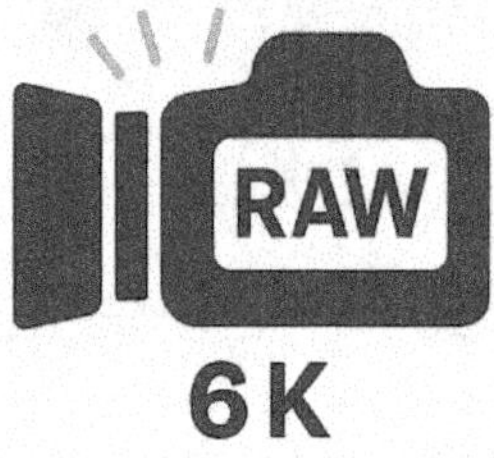

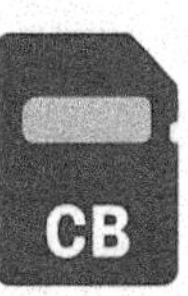

COOLING, CODECS & CARD WORKFLOW EXPLAINED

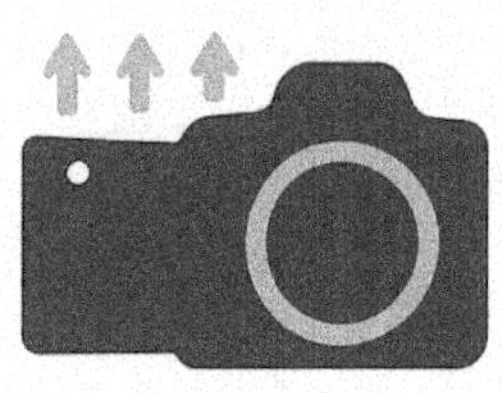

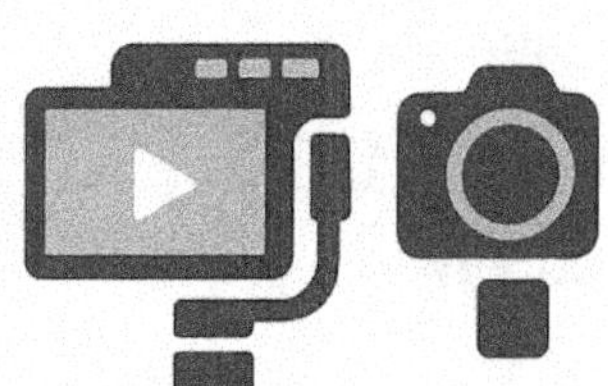

Hybrid Rig Builds: Tripod, Gimbal, Handhelheld

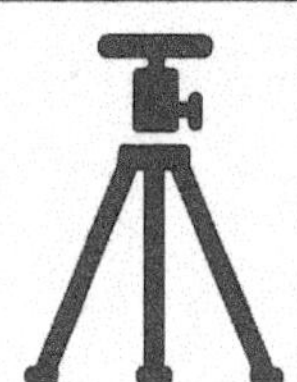

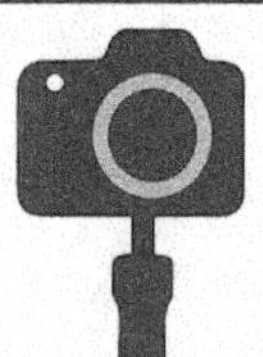

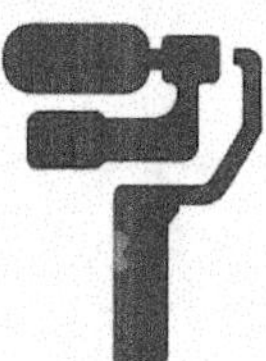

Part V: Workflow & Longevity

Chapter 12

Building an Efficient Workflow

When you're working with a flagship like the EOS R1, capturing extraordinary moments is only half the story. The other half—and just as critical—is how you move, safeguard, and process those files. Professional workflow isn't about gear for its own sake; it's about speed, reliability, and ensuring nothing gets lost when the stakes are highest. In this chapter, we'll break down tethering, FTP, and cloud solutions; strategies for organizing and naming files; and battle-tested backup habits that keep your work bulletproof, even on the road.

Tethering, FTP Transfer & Cloud Solutions

Tethering for Studio & Controlled Shoots

For fashion, portrait, and commercial work, tethering is the gold standard. The EOS R1's high-speed USB-C port lets you shoot directly to a laptop running software like Capture One or Canon's EOS Utility. This not only provides instant previews on a large screen but also reduces card swaps. Tethering is best when:

- Clients need live feedback.

- You're color-grading on set.

- Critical sharpness must be checked before talent leaves.

FTP for Real-Time Delivery

Sports photographers and photojournalists rely on FTP to move files the second they're captured. The R1 can push selected JPEGs or RAWs straight to an FTP server or editor's desk, whether you're courtside or in a stadium press box. Pro tip:

- Configure custom "Send to FTP" buttons, so you can transmit winning shots while still tracking the play.

- Use dual cards: one for immediate FTP transmission (JPEGs), one for full RAW archival.

Cloud Integration

For freelancers or hybrid shooters, Canon's image.canon and third-party cloud services like Dropbox or Frame.io bridge field work with postproduction. Imagine a wedding photographer shooting all day, with key images already uploading to the cloud via Wi-Fi before the reception ends. When you get home, they're waiting, organized, and synced across devices.

File Naming, Card Strategy & On-the-Road

Backup

File Naming Conventions

Sloppy file names are workflow poison. Establish a system that codes date, project, and camera body. Example:

- `2025-08-18_Wedding_Smith_R1A_001.CR3`
- `2025-08-18_Wedding_Smith_R1B_001.CR3`

  This prevents overlaps when you're shooting with multiple bodies and makes retrieval painless.

Card Strategy

- **Use Pro-Grade CFexpress Cards**: Stick with brands tested for reliability. Saving a few dollars isn't worth risking a corrupt buffer.

- **Dual Card Redundancy**: One card records RAW, the other records JPEG or RAW mirror for insurance.

- **Rotate & Label**: Number your cards physically (1, 2, 3…). After a shoot, retire them to a "used" case until offloaded. Never mix "used" and "fresh" cards in your pocket.

Backup on the Road

Three is the magic number for pros:

1. Primary copy – on your cards until you verify transfer.

2. Secondary copy – on a laptop or portable SSD.

3. Tertiary copy – on a second SSD or portable backup system (e.g., GNARBOX or Nexto DI).

If you're traveling internationally, keep one backup physically separated—luggage or hotel safe—so theft or loss doesn't wipe everything.

Building Workflow Habits That Last

Even with all the tech, the real difference comes down to consistency. The most efficient shooters don't waste energy reinventing workflow every assignment. Instead, they have checklists:

- Always rename on ingest.

- Always duplicate before formatting.

- Always confirm backups before sleep.

The EOS R1 provides speed and reliability in the field. Your workflow should mirror that same philosophy—fast, predictable, and bulletproof.

Field Takeaway: A flagship body earns its worth not only in the frames it captures but in the confidence it gives you that no frame will ever be lost. Treat your workflow like part of your kit. Just as you wouldn't step into a stadium with uncharged batteries, don't walk into an assignment with a messy, untested file strategy.

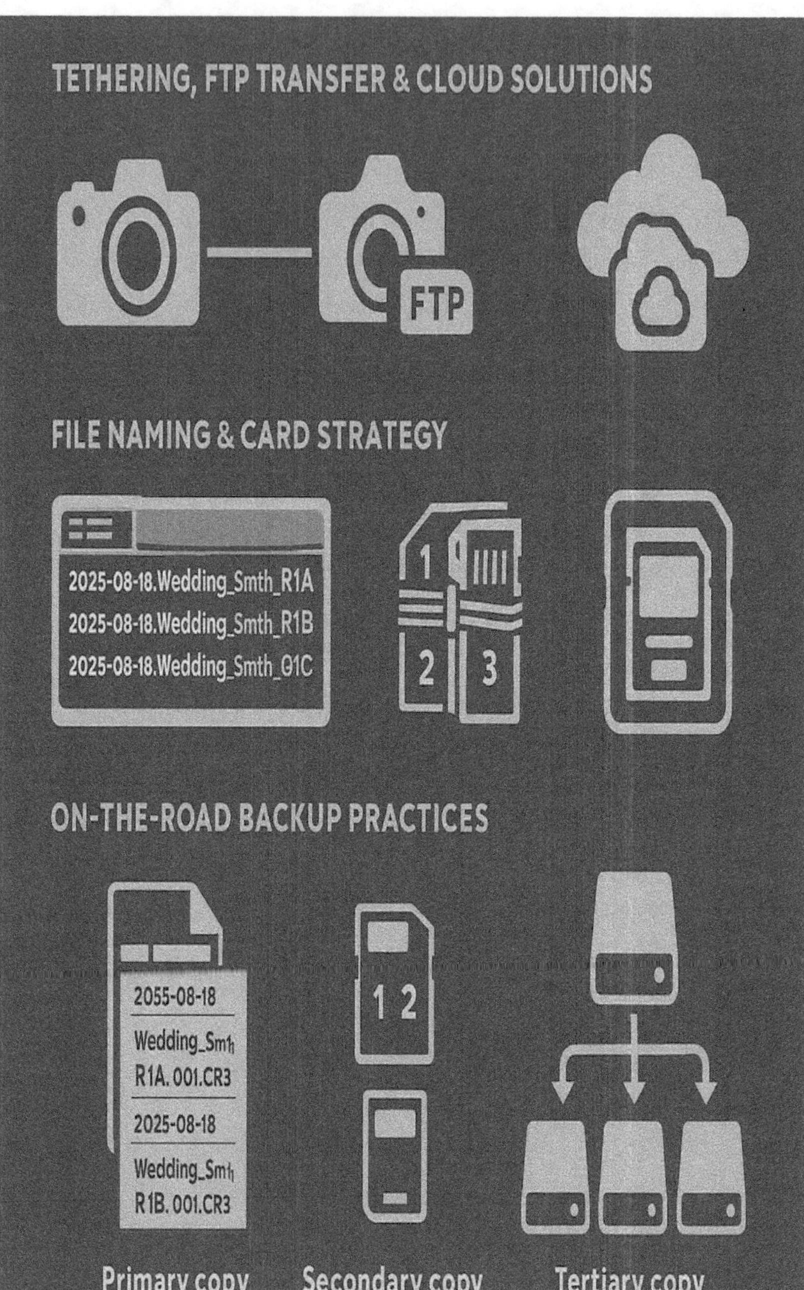

TETHERING, FTP TRANSFER & CLOUD SOLUTIONS
FTP
FILE NAMING & CARD STRATEGY
2025-08-18.Wedding_Smth_R1A
2025-08-18.Wedding_Smth_R1B
2025-08-18.Wedding_Smth_01C
1
2 3
ON-THE-ROAD BACKUP PRACTICES
2055-08-18
Wedding_Smth
R1A. 001.CR3
2025-08-18
Wedding_Smth
R1B. 001.CR3
1 2
Primary copy
Secondary copy
Tertiary copy

Chapter 13

Firmware, Future-Proofing & Staying Ahead

Every flagship camera is more than the sum of its launch-day specifications. Canon's R1 is a platform—engineered not just for the present but for the future. The DNA inside this body reflects years of Canon's pro philosophy, but the real secret is how the camera continues to evolve long after you've unboxed it. Firmware, settings retention, and smart upgrade habits determine whether your R1 feels like a timeless tool or an outdated piece of gear within a few years.

This chapter is your blueprint for future-proofing the R1 so it serves you reliably across seasons, genres, and the inevitable march of new technology.

Updating Without Losing Settings

One of the quiet frustrations for professionals is the risk of losing carefully dialed-in setups after a firmware update. Your R1 allows for safe updating, but only if you prepare properly.

Here's the golden rule: Back up before you update.

- Use Custom Settings Backup: On your R1, you can save entire menu maps and custom button assignments to your memory card. This means that even if the firmware resets some behaviors, you can reload your personal workflow in seconds.

- Dual Card Safety: Always perform updates with one card dedicated to the firmware file and keep the other slot empty—or holding your setup backup. This prevents accidental overwrites.

- Stable Power Source: Never update on a half-drained battery. Use a fully charged Canon-branded battery or AC adapter to avoid mid-update crashes that could brick your system.

With this workflow, updating becomes stress-free, not a gamble.

New Firmware Features Explained

Canon treats the R1 as a living system. Expect firmware updates not just for bug fixes but for performance enhancements. This is where the camera stretches beyond its launch-day promise.

Some categories of updates you can expect:

- Autofocus Refinements: Canon often adds new subject detection types (e.g., birds, motorcycles, airplanes) or improves eye-tracking speed.

- Video Enhancements: Extra codecs, expanded frame-rate options, or heat management tweaks.

- Connectivity & Workflow: Smarter FTP transfer, cloud integration, or compatibility with new tethering standards.

- Bug Fixes & Stability: Small but essential—resolving menu lag, memory card communication issues, or rare AF glitches.

Tip: Canon posts firmware changelogs online. Print them or save them to a workflow folder on your computer. After each update, spend 15 minutes with the camera testing the "new toys" before a real job. This ensures you know what changed—and whether it helps or alters your usual recipes.

Staying Ahead of the Curve

Technology moves fast, but the R1 is engineered as a long-term body, not a quick turnover like prosumer models. The reasons are clear:

- Pro Build Quality: Weather sealing, reinforced shutter, magnesium alloy body—designed for a decade of work.

- Processor Power: Canon packs the R1 with processing headroom; firmware unlocks more of it over time.

- Lens Ecosystem: RF lenses are Canon's long game; your R1 is a hub that will only grow more capable as optics evolve.

- Pro Support & Service: Canon CPS (Canon Professional Services) ensures parts, repairs, and priority servicing—an assurance for those building careers around this camera.

Instead of asking, *"When should I replace my R1?"*, ask: *"How can I keep this body running at peak?"* The truth: the R1 is likely to outlive your creative cycles if you maintain firmware discipline and treat it as a platform rather than a gadget.

The Professional's Perspective

Owning an R1 is less about chasing the next upgrade and more about extracting the full potential of the one you already have. Each firmware update is like a free gift of extra horsepower. Each backup routine preserves your craft against accidental resets. Each new lens release pushes the body's capabilities further into the future.

The R1 is your long-term creative partner. Learn to nurture it, keep it current, and it will reward you with years of reliability across sports fields, wildlife reserves, wedding aisles, and film sets.

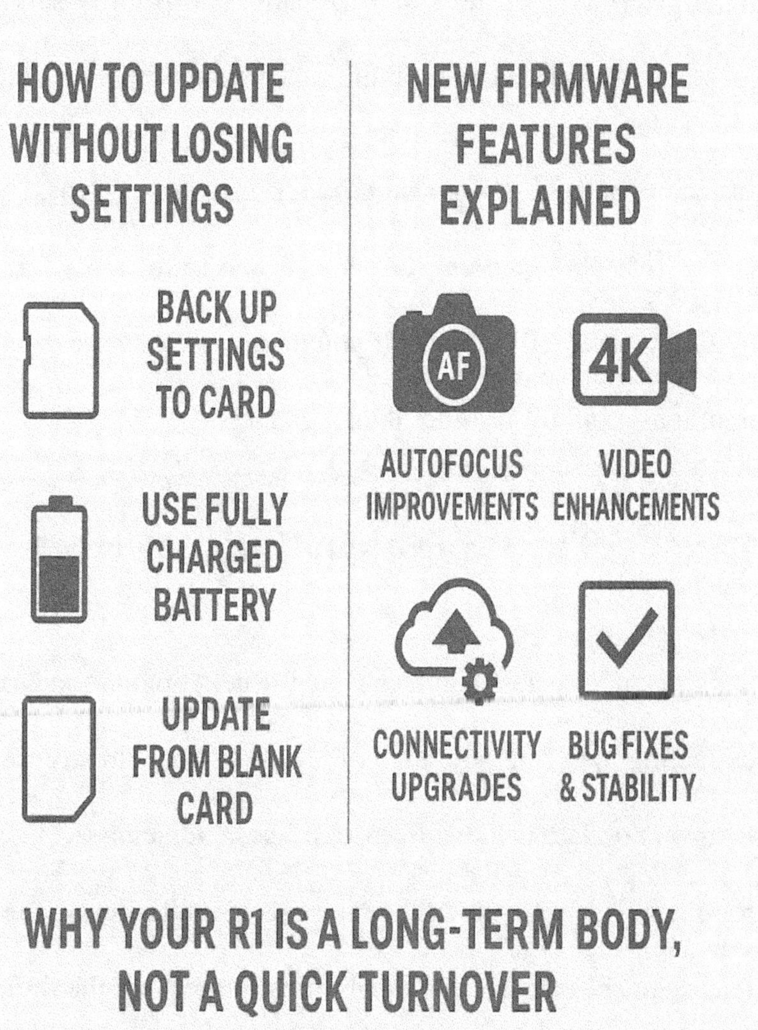

Bonus

Quick-Reference Field Cards –

Settings Recipes by Scenario

The Canon EOS R1 is a powerhouse, but when you're under pressure in the field, remembering every fine detail isn't always possible. These quick-reference "field cards" distill the setups we've covered throughout the book into fast, scenario-based recipes you can glance at before a shoot or even screenshot to keep on your phone.

Sports – Indoor Basketball (Fast, Erratic Movement, Harsh Lighting)

- **AF Case:** Case 2 (tracking sensitivity lowered slightly to hold subjects)

- **AF Method:** Flexible Zone AF + Eye Detection

- **Drive Mode:** High-speed burst (20–30 fps, depending on card capacity)

- **ISO:** Auto ISO with upper limit set to 6400

- **Shutter Speed:** Lock at 1/1000s or higher

- **Lens Choice:** 70–200mm f/2.8 or 135mm f/1.8

Wildlife – Birds in Flight

- **AF Case:** Case 3 (aggressive tracking for sudden movements)

- **AF Method:** Whole Area with Subject Detection set to Animals

- **Drive Mode:** Maximum burst (30 fps+) with Pre-Shoot Burst engaged

- **Shutter Speed:** 1/2500s minimum

- **ISO:** Auto with upper limit ~10,000 (accept noise, get the shot)

- **Lens Choice:** 400mm f/2.8, 600mm f/4, or 100–500mm for mobility

Events – Wedding Portraits

- **AF Case:** Case 1 (general)

- **AF Method:** Eye Detection for single subject → switch to Group Detection for family shots

- **Exposure Mode:** Manual with Auto ISO

- **ISO:** Keep under 3200 for cleaner skin tones

- **Lens Choice:** 50mm f/1.2 for portraits, 24–70mm f/2.8 for groups

- **Note:** Pre-program custom buttons for quick AF swaps

Documentary/News – One-Chance Capture

- **AF Case:** Case 2 (stable tracking)

- **AF Method:** Flexible Zone + Eye Detection fallback

- **Drive Mode:** Medium burst (don't flood your buffer too quickly)

- **ISO:** Auto with cap at 12,800

- **Workflow:** Dual card slots (RAW + JPEG to separate cards for redundancy)

Glossary of Key Terms

AF Case: Canon's preset autofocus response behaviors (e.g., how quickly the system reacts to subject movement or interference). Think of them as "personalities" for the AF system.

Buffer: The camera's internal memory that temporarily holds images before writing to the memory card. Once full, your shooting speed slows down.

Dual Pixel CMOS AF II: Canon's advanced autofocus system where every pixel on the sensor doubles as an AF point.

Eye-Controlled AF: A unique Canon system that detects where your eye looks in the viewfinder and shifts focus accordingly.

Highlight Alert ("Blinkies"): Flashing highlights in playback that warn you when parts of the image are overexposed.

Pre-Shoot Burst: A buffer-based feature that records a fraction of a second before you fully press the shutter—useful for unpredictable action.

Zebra Patterns: Striped overlays that appear on overexposed areas during video or live view, helping you protect highlights.

Resources & Recommended Accessories

Owning the EOS R1 is just the beginning—your system grows stronger with reliable accessories and workflow tools.

Memory Cards

- CFexpress Type B: For maximum speed in 6K RAW and 30 fps bursts. Brands like ProGrade Digital or Sony Tough are battle-tested.

- SD UHS-II: Use as secondary storage or backup; not fast enough for the R1's highest modes.

Batteries & Power

- Canon LP-E19: The official high-capacity pack for the R1. Keep at least two spares.
- USB-C PD Power Banks: Essential for long wildlife or documentary shoots where outlets are scarce.

Stabilization

- Professional Gimbal (DJI RS3 Pro or similar): For video or fast-moving documentary work.
- Carbon-fiber monopod: The balance between mobility and stability for sports/wildlife.

Audio (for Video Shooters)

- Canon DM-E1D digital mic (hot-shoe powered, clean digital signal).

146

- Wireless lavalier system (RØDE, Sennheiser, or DJI) for interviews and documentary setups.

Software & Cloud

- Canon EOS Utility: For tethering and remote shooting.

- Capture One / Lightroom: For RAW processing and color workflows.

- Canon Image.Canon Cloud: Simple auto-backup solution on the road.

Final Note to the Reader

This guide was built to go beyond the dry manuals—to serve as a working companion. Keep experimenting, keep pushing your R1, and keep refining your own recipes in the field. The more you shoot, the more the camera adapts to you, becoming less a tool and more an extension of your vision.

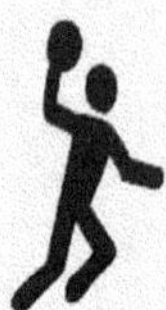 Sports – Indoor Basketball	Wildlife – Birds in Flight
• **AF Case:** Case 2 • **AF Method:** Flexible Zone + Eye Detection • **Drive Mode:** High-speed burst • **ISO:** Auto, limit 6400 • **Shutter Speed:** 1/100s or faster	• **AF Case:** Case 3 • **AF Method:** Whole Area + Subject Detection • **Drive Mode:** Maximum burst • **ISO:** Auto, limit 10,000 • **Lens Choice:** 400 mm f/2.8 600 mm f/4, or 100–500 mm
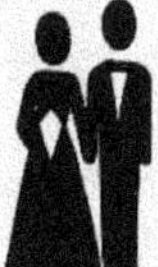 Events – Wedding Portraits	Documentary/News – One-Chance Capture
• **AF Case:** Case 1 • **AF Method:** Eye Detection → Group Detection • **Exposure Mode:** Manual + Auto ISO • **ISO:** <3200 • **Lens** Choice: 50mm f/.2 or 24–30 mm f/2.8	• **AF Case:** Case 2 • **AF Method:** Flexible Zone + Eye Detection • **Drive Mode:** Medium burst • **ISO:** Auto, limit 12,800 • **Workflow:** Dual cards

Acknowledgments

Creating this guide has been a journey made possible by more than just technical know-how—it's been powered by community, curiosity, and countless moments behind the lens.

First, to the everyday photographers—beginners, seniors, travelers, vloggers, and creators—who inspired this book: thank you. Your questions, frustrations, and breakthroughs shaped every chapter and reminded me why clarity matters.

To the online communities, forum contributors, and real-world Canon EOS R1 users who openly shared their challenges and insights: your stories breathed realism into this work.

A special thanks to my editorial team, design collaborators, and research assistants for helping bring structure, precision, and visual support to every page.

Finally, to the readers picking up this book—whether you're just unboxing your Canon R1 or finally ready to leave auto mode behind—thank you for trusting this guide as part of your journey. May it help you create images that not only look beautiful, but feel meaningful.

Keep shooting. Keep learning. The world is waiting through your lens.

About The Author

Randy Osborn is a trusted name in the world of camera education, known for transforming complex gear manuals into simple, step-by-step guides that anyone can understand. With over a decade of experience working hands-on with leading camera systems—from Sony and Canon to Nikon, Leica, and more—Randy has helped thousands of photographers, content creators, and everyday users get the most out of their cameras without the overwhelm.

Driven by a passion for accessible learning, Randy creates user-friendly books that strip away the jargon and focus on real-world usage. Whether you're shooting your first vlog, learning manual mode for the first time, or simply trying to take better family photos, Randy's guides are designed to make every setting click.

Each book combines clear instruction, practical tips, and

relatable language, making it easy for beginners and seasoned hobbyists alike to master their gear and capture life with confidence.

When he's not writing, Randy enjoys field testing new camera releases, hosting beginner-friendly workshops, and exploring hidden photography gems across the globe.

Join the journey to sharper skills and smarter shooting—one page at a time.